ALSATIAN AUTONOMIST LEADERS
1919 - 1947

Alsatian Autonomist Leaders
1919 - 1947

PHILIP CHARLES FARWELL BANKWITZ

The Regents Press of Kansas
Lawrence

Library of Congress Cataloging in Publication Data
Bankwitz, Philip Charles Farwell.
Alsatian autonomist leaders, 1919–1947.

Bibliography: p.
Includes index.
1. Alsace—History—Autonomy and independence movements.
I. Title.
DC650.5.B36   944'.383'081   77-10665
ISBN 0-7006-0160-0

To

Madame Marguerite Hauth-Boeckel

*Alsatian of ancient lineage, faithful friend,
and wise counsellor*

Vous n'aurez pas l'Alsace et la Lorraine
Et malgré vous, nous resterons français!
Vous pouvez bien germaniser la plaine,
Mais notre coeur vous ne l'aurez jamais.

O Strassburg, O Strassburg
Du wunderschöne Stadt,
Darinnen liegt begraben
So manicher Soldat.

So mancher und schöner,
Auch tapferer Soldat,
Der Vater und lieb Mutter
Böslich verlassen hat.

Verlassen, verlassen,
Es kann nicht anders sein!
Zu Strassburg, ja zu Strassburg
Soldaten müssen sein.

Der Vater, die Mutter
Die gingen vors Hauptmanns Haus:
"Ach Hauptmann, lieber Herr Hauptmann,"
"Gebt mir mein'n Sohn heraus."

"Euern Sohn kann ich nicht geben
für noch so vieles Geld.
Euer Sohn und der muss sterben
Im weit und breiten Feld."

O Elsass unser Landl,
Dis isch mainaidi schoen!
Mer hewe's fescht am Bandl,
Un lon's bi Gott net gehn!
Juchhe!
Un lon's bi Gott net gehn!

Contents

Contents

Acknowledgments

I am indebted to the American Council of Learned Societies, the Fondation Camargo, my parents, and Trinity College for funding my research and enabling me to write this book. I am especially grateful to Michel Debré and René Pleven, former French ministers of national defense and of justice, respectively, for having authorized access to the documents on which this study is based. For their invaluable help, I would also like to thank Mr. Chaussavoine of the Dépôt Central d'Archives de la Justice militaire; Pierre Gérard, director of the Archives de Meurthe-et-Moselle; Christian Wilsdorf, director of the Archives du Haut-Rhin; and François-Joseph Himly, director of the Archives du Bas-Rhin. Without the selfless aid of many—André Bord, secretary of state to the minister of the interior; Guy Sautter, general councillor of Bas-Rhin; Jean Verdier, prefect of the region of Alsace and of Bas-Rhin; Gen. Vernon Walters, military attaché, U.S. Embassy in Paris; Roger Masters and Russell Harris, cultural attachés of the U.S. Embassy in Paris; and Général Paul Stehlin—the writing of this book would have been impossible.

Prof. Hans-Adolf Jacobsen of the University of Bonn, Prof. Thilo Vogelsang of the Institut für Zeitgeschichte, Messrs. Michewski, Henke, and Reise of the Bundesarchiv in Coblenz, and Ursula Bodenburg of the Auswärtiges Amt in Bonn all were instrumental in securing my access to the pertinent German documents. Prof. Leslie Derfler of Florida Atlantic University and Prof. Stewart Doty of the University of Maine were of great help in alerting me to Alexandre Millerand's and Maurice Barrès's contributions to modern Alsatian history. Henri Michel and Marthe Clauser of the Comité d'histoire de la 2e. guerre mondiale gave invaluable help in the documentation of this book. I should also like to mention my good and faithful friend, Prof. William E. Scott of Duke University, who was of invaluable assistance in bringing this book into print. Finally, I would like to thank my friends in Alsace—Jean Degermann, Edouard Degott, Roger Muller, George-Charles Bené, and Jean-Pierre Heyler and his parents—for their devotion and inspiration at critical moments.

Introduction

In preparing this study of five modern Alsatian autonomist leaders—Joseph Victor Rossé, Jean-Pierre Mourer, Marcel Stürmel, Hermann Bickler, and Friedrich Spieser—I have not attempted a history of the autonomist movement itself nor an analysis of the region or economy of Alsace. The reason lies in the nature of the documentation presently available. Judicial and national defense records dealing with the Alsatian autonomist leaders are now open to researchers on a limited basis, but party records, membership lists, transcripts of meetings, prefectoral reports, and other information on the various groups involved in the Alsatian autonomist movement—materials housed in the rich F^7 series of the Ministry of the Interior archives—are still closed. I have, therefore, only sketched the movement to set the stage for the appearance of the autonomist leaders during the hectic and important decade of the 1920s.

Along with the five autonomist leaders, I have chosen to discuss in some detail two other figures important to the movement. They are Robert Wagner, who was *Gauleiter* ("district leader") of Alsace during the German occupation from 1940 to 1945, and Robert Ernst, who was, during the 1920s and 1930s, the primary conduit through whom German funds were funneled to the autonomist leaders.

This study does not pretend to be a history of autonomism as seen through the local and international press, although when pertinent—for example, in discussing the trials of the autonomist leaders—I have used press reports. (Readers interested in the autonomist press during the 1920s, should consult the excellent work done by students of Prof. Fernand L'Huillier at the University of Strasbourg.) Finally, interviews with autonomist leaders provided only a minor part of the information presented here. The reason is simple: by the time I began to work on this project in the early 1970s, all of the leaders except Marcel Stürmel were either dead or in hiding.

This analysis is clearly a study of failure. The autonomist leaders could not achieve their goal of a self-governing Alsace, balanced between two powerful neighbors. The obstacles were too great: the years from 1919 to 1947 were an era of perfervid nationalism, of highly centralized nation-states fighting two total wars against one another within thirty years. But the fact that Rossé, Mourer, Stürmel, Bickler, and Spieser tried to achieve their aims is an illustration of the tenacity—some would say sheer stubbornness—which has always characterized the inhabitants of this beguiling land between the Vosges and the Rhine. The fact that their efforts ended in the nightmare of Nazi occupation from 1940 to 1945 does not diminish the importance of these Alsatians in the modern history of Franco-German relations and of autonomism in general.

ALSATIAN AUTONOMIST LEADERS
1919 - 1947

Abbreviations

A.P.N.A.: Action Populaire Nationale d'Alsace
DAI: Deutsches Auslands-Institut Stuttgart
E.L.Z.: Elsass-Lothringische Zeitung
*J. O. C. Débs.: Journal officiel de la république française
1870–1940, Chambre des députés, 1876–1940, Débats parlementaires. Compte rendu in extenso, 11 janvier 1881–4 juin 1940*
*J. O. S. Débs.: Journal officiel de la république française,
1870–1940, Senat, 1876–1940, Débats parlementaires, Compte rendu in extenso, 11 janvier 1881–21 mai 1940*
NSDAP: Nationalsozialistische Deutsche Arbeiterpartei
RSHA: Reichssicherheitshauptamt
SD: Sicherheitsdienst
SA: Sturmabteilung
SiPo: Sicherheitspolizei
SS: Schutzstaffel
U.P.R.: Union Populaire Républicaine
V.D.A.: Verein für das Deutschtum im Ausland

1

Autonomism before 1919

Alsace, an area of just over three thousand square miles, is primarily an agricultural region, known in particular for its white wines. Tucked between the Vosges Mountains and the upper Rhine River, Alsace is bordered by Germany to the north and east, France (and the region of Lorraine) to the west, and Switzerland to the south. (Lorraine is not covered in this study. It has been associated with Alsace only in recent times, since Germany annexed the northeast portion—the former French department of Moselle—in 1871.) The Alsatians are an essentially Alemmanic people, mixed with earlier strains of Celts, Gauls, and Romans and a later one of Franks.[1] While their language and customs link them to the Swiss Germans and the Baden Germans, their political culture derives from the French Revolution. Of all the peoples of ancient Lotharingia, the Alsatians were the ones most closely tied to the revolution in its original sense: the constitution of 1791, not the Jacobin Terror, the Thermidorean settlement, and the subsequent Napoleonic centralization. In fact, modern Alsatian relations with France (out of which sprang the autonomist leaders analyzed in this study) can be seen, in part, as a struggle to reassert the principles of the great federation that came together on the Champs de Mars in Paris on July 14, 1790.

3

This struggle ended in failure: the Alsatians, as a frontier people in modern times, have never been given autonomy in its true sense either by France (1919–39, 1945–) or by Germany (1870–1919, 1939–45). The reason is simple: as all analyses of nationalism show, cultural particularism often undermines the state and leads to political separatism.[2] But despite their having been shuttled between French and German poles for the past thousand years, the Alsatians retain the vivacity, individualism, and distinctiveness of a true border people. Their predicament is perhaps best summed up in the motto of their eighteenth century cardinal-princes— the Rohans—who, as transplanted Bretons, were immediately sympathetic to Alsatian aspirations:

Français ne puis-je,
Allemand ne daigne,
Alsacien suis-je.

French I cannot be
German I disdain to be,
Alsatian am I.

The modern interwar autonomist movement was actually, as the period's leading political analyst, François G. Dreyfus, has put it, "three autonomies." One was Catholic and not necessarily anti-French; it was concentrated in the French department of Haut-Rhin (southern Alsace). The second, in Bas-Rhin (northern Alsace), was lay and liberal and desired to remain within the French political framework. The third, overtly anti-French and separatist, was located in the Protestant communes along the northern, Palatinate border and in the extension of Alsace west beyond Niederbronn and Bouxwiller (called "crooked Alsace").

The historical background of modern autonomism in Alsace in both rich and extensive. Freedom from central control has always been an important element in Alsatian history. During the Middle Ages, Strasbourg was a free city as were the members of the League of the Ten Alsatian Imperial Cities; during the Renaissance, the Swiss canton of Mulhouse and the Estates of Upper and Lower Alsace arose. Later, under the French *ancien régime*, a bewildering mélange of economic, political, and social privileges given to princes, lords, corporations, cities, and religious groups effectively made Alsace before 1789 a foreign province.[3] Its customs frontier was on the Vosges, its Catholic clergy was separate from that of the rest of France, and its nobility was oriented toward the Holy Roman Empire. "Do not disturb the rights of Alsace" (*Ne pas toucher aux choses de l'Alsace*) was the maxim of the Bourbon kings and their administrators.[4] In fact, even the integrative centralization of the French Revolution's Jacobin and Napoleonic periods could not obliterate the special provincial characteristics of language, religion, morals, and customs which made one French observer in the mid-nineteenth century term Alsace "German France."[5]

Modern Alsatian autonomism appeared as early as the first French defeats of the Franco-Prussian War, in August 1870, and with the first rumors of the region's annexation by Germany. At Bordeaux, on February 17 and March 1, 1871, a united front of provincial deputies protested before the French National Assembly the cession to Germany of the departments of Moselle (Lorraine), Bas-Rhin, and Haut-Rhin (Alsace). The deputies were backed by at least three outspoken autonomists —Frédéric Hartmann, Auguste Schneegans, and Emile Küss—who were determined to see the region independent, balanced between victorious Germany and defeated France.[6] Prominent Alsatians, such as Hartmann, Ignace Chauffour, Jules Klein, and Jacques Kablé, sought to soften the blow of separation from France by advocating an autonomous status that would include a bilingual educational system, administrative independence, and a plebiscite to let the region's inhabitants decide whether to belong to the old country or to Germany.[7]

Instead, Bismarck created the Reichsland out of the three annexed departments, the "province of the new German Empire," headed by a "supreme president" who could, if necessary, exercise state-of-seige military powers. The new subjects of the German emperor immediately dubbed this authorization the "dictatorship paragraph."[8] Nevertheless, autonomism did not die: it became part of the protest against annexation (*protestation*), the dominant political element of the early 1870s, and embraced demands for a plebiscite (*abstention*). (The term *abstention* derives from an 1874 speech before the Reichstag by Eduard Teutsch of Saverne, in which he demanded that Alsatians "be called upon to decide in a special way" whether or not to accept their incorporation into the Reich, a move taken "without their consent.")[9]

By the end of the decade, Bismarck saw in autonomism a possible way to reconcile Alsatians to their fate. In 1879 he made important concessions, abolishing the supreme president and establishing instead a *Statthalter* ("lieutenant") aided by two assemblies. One, the Délégation (Landesauschuss), was chosen from the local Alsatian assemblies; the other was an appointed Council of State. Legislative power for the region was conferred on the Landesauschuss and on the Reichstag (to which Alsace had sent delegates since 1874), but the Reichsland was denied representation in the upper house of the German national assembly, the Bundesrat. Bismarck's efforts were successful; the protest movement eventually discarded demands for a plebiscite in favor of greater representation and freedom within the Second German Empire.

Under the first of Alsace's German governors, Gen. Edwin von Manteuffel, significant changes began to take place. Taking advantage of the Treaty of Frankfurt's "option" provisions (which allowed those who wished to preserve their French citizenship to leave Alsace before October 1, 1872, and reside in France), more than fifty thousand French sympathizers, drawn mostly from the rural and urban intellectual elite, left the region immediately after the Franco-Prussian War. In addition, there was a massive influx of citizens from the Reich; by 1910 some four hundred thousand Germans were living in Alsace. With these demographic shifts came political realignments. The united front of Liberal Democrats and Catholics—the "protesters"—began to disintegrate. Despite several serious crises, including the war scare of 1881 with the Gambetta ministry in France and the German reaction between 1884 and 1887, the first elections favorable to the Germans took place in 1893. That year four "protesters" were elected to the Reichstag as against five governmental deputies, two of whom (Pöhlmann of Sélestat and Hohenlohe-Schillingfurst of Hagenau-Wissembourg) were Germans.[10]

During the late 1890s, with the appearance of a new generation, a new era of Alsatian politics began. The old "protesters" were replaced by autonomists of various allegiances—Catholic Zentrum, Social Democrats, Liberals—working no longer through the original Landesauschuss, but within the German parliamentary system. The empire was, at least in theory, a federal state. Consequently, with the 1902 abolition of the Statthalter's extraordinary state-of-seige powers, the goal of autonomism became to obtain for Alsace the status of a German *Land* ("state"). The *Länder* not only were represented in the Bundesrat, but in peacetime, enjoyed considerable independence through control of direct taxes, as well as control of the police, the judiciary, and the educational system. (In fact, Bavaria, the largest of the German states, was allowed its own army and diplomatic service.)[11]

Land status was the goal on which all autonomists agreed however much they differed over what autonomy meant, be it universal suffrage, full Alsatian sovereignty, a republic, Alsatian "originality," reconciliation of Alsatians, French, and Germans, or even eventual integration into the Second Reich.[12] Under the urging of Graf von Wedel, the Statthalter appointed in 1907, who prodded Reichstag, chancellor, and emperor alike, an Alsatian constitution was drawn up in 1911, satisfying some, enraging others. On the one hand, like Baden, Alsace was given representation in the Bundesrat, and a provincial parliament (Landtag) made up of an elected lower chamber of sixty deputies and an upper house of forty-one appointed representatives. On the other hand, selection of the three Bundesrat representatives was left to a non-Alsatian, the Statthalter. The Landtag shared its legislative powers with the Statthalter, particularly during parliamentary recesses and in case of delays on the budget vote. In addition, Germans were appointed to a disproportionately high number of seats in the upper house of the Landtag.[13] The new law, then, did not define Alsatian nationality nor did it make Alsace a *Land* of comparable autonomy to the other German states.[14] In response, a *Nationalbund* ("national alliance")—a precedecessor of the Heimatbund of 1926— immediately emerged, pointing the way toward a true Alsatian national party by insisting on equality for Alsace and free development of Alsatian individuality within the empire. In both chambers of the Landtag, the battle for autonomism began "under the triple sign of demands for an official place for the Church, a program of democracy, and [a] rejection of Germanism."[15]

In short, what the Germans gave Alsace with one

hand, they took back with the other. Two incidents symbolize the restlessness of the province and the fact that after two generations, the Alsatians were still not reconciled to German rule. The first, in the spring of 1912, involved the forced resignation of Théophile Heyler, director of the region's important locomotive works in Graffenstaden. Heyler was accused of pro-French sympathies by the powerful organ of rival Ruhr industrial interests, the *Rheinisch-westfälische Zeitung*. Despite a resolution of the Alsatian Landtag condemning the German official responsible (Under-Secretary of the Interior Mandel), Heyler was forced to resign and was replaced by a German.[16] The second incident was much more notorious. In November 1913, a young Prussian officer, Lieutenant von Forstner, of the Saverne garrison insulted his Alsatian conscripts, the French Foreign Legion, and the French flag and beat a crippled shoemaker. (Forstner used the pejorative word *wackes* [bums] to describe his Alsatian recruits.) When Bethmann-Hollweg defended von Forstner and the other officers involved, the Alsatian deputies in the Reichstag obtained a motion to censure the German chancellor. The result, however, was simply the removal of the only Alsatian in the Reichsland government.[17]

Alsace drifted into the First World War firmly under the control of its German masters. Recovery of the region had long since ceased to be an objective of French foreign policy.[18] The "lost provinces" were merely a sentimental element in the French national consciousness, kept alive by folklore, the novels of Erckmann-Chatrian, Hervé Bazin, and Maurice Barrès, and the anti-German caricatures of "Hansi" (Jean-Jacques Waltz) and Henri Zislin. The cruel and patronizing treatment of Alsatians in France as portrayed in Sartre's *Les mots* is all too clear on this point.[19]

With the declaration of war, Alsace fell under Ger-

man military dictatorship: as the autonomist artist and
writer Charles Spindler observed in 1914, nine weeks
of the wartime regime destroyed forty-four years of
German administrative accomplishment. Thann and
Dannemarie (Haut-Rhin) were occupied by the French
from the beginning of the war; one of the most vicious
battles of the great holocaust was fought on the Hart-
mannswillerkopf in the same region. The number of
evacuations, arrests, internments, and expulsions—esti-
mated at three to four thousand—did little to improve
Alsatians' feelings toward the German military.[20] In
addition, the Germans still had to contend with autonomism. On June 12, 1917, Dr. Georges Ricklin, president of the Landtag, issued a declaration insisting on
Land status for Alsace. Six months later, the report of
the Statthalter emphasized the strength of the autonomist
idea while concluding that Alsace should become part
of Prussia (thus echoing earlier German annexationist
designs in northeastern France and Belgium).[21]

As the war's end drew near, full autonomy with an
Alsatian Statthalter was finally granted by Chancellor
Max von Baden on October 14, 1918. But by this time,
the province and its parliament were rife with demands
for a confederated neutral state, or a free and neutral
republic, or a return to France. The days of the empire
were past; its "cement," the Reichsland, was crumbling.[22]
In effect, the note of the Entente powers, dated January
10, 1917, had given France the region. Furthermore, the
eighth of Wilson's Fourteen Points demanded the return
of Alsace-Lorraine to France. As a modest workers' and
soldiers' revolution began in Strasbourg on November
9, 1918, and with the Landtag transforming itself into a
National Council three days later, would Spindler's
confident prediction come true? Would the Alsatians
abandon regionalism in favor of rapid assimilation with
France?[23]

2

Autonomism, 1919 - 1939

The Alsatians who had been "exiles" in France since 1871 and the entire French army were astounded by the wildly enthusiastic welcome accorded them by the "lost province" in November and December 1918.[1] At the Hotel de Ville in Strasbourg on December 9, President Raymond Poincaré declared, *"Le plebiscite est fait* (the plebiscite has been decided)": Alsace returned to France with genuine joy.

But France was no longer the Catholic, regionalist-minded country of 1870; it had become the secular, centralized Third Republic. The region of Alsace was given a high commissioner, but one whose powers were far fewer than those of the Statthalter. The Landtag passed out of existence on January 14, 1919, and was not replaced by a French version of the provincial assembly. The communications network in Alsace, as well as the region's water and forestry departments, were directly controlled from Paris. Special commissions were set up to classify the population according to nationality: these *commissions de triage* divided the inhabitants of Alsace according to whether they were of German, Alsatian, or mixed parentage. This classification, which severely limited the rights and privileges of all but pure-bred Alsatians, was later described by Robert Redslob, dean of the University of Strasbourg and a renowned professor of international law, as "an antijuridical conception."[2] The places held by departing Germans in the local administration were taken by officials "from the interior," who could understand neither German nor the regional dialect; Alsatian functionaries were passed over. The difficulties of language compounded the problems of reunion: many Alsatian teachers were forced to take French lessons to continue working in the schools, and controversies soon arose over when and how to begin teaching French, the region's new official language.

Under the circumstances, it is not surprising that autonomism revived. Gone were the days when speakers, addressing huge throngs in Strasbourg, appealed in the native dialect for the "expulsion of all elements of pure German nationality," arguing, "We wish no longer to live with a nation . . . which subjugated us. Long live the Allies!"[3] The autonomist movement had been born: the first indication was a general strike against French "assimilation" called by Alsatian teachers and bureaucrats on April 20, 1920. This demonstration was first barred and then broken up by the French police.

Some of the early postwar autonomists were inoffensive and even faintly comic. For example, in 1919, members of the Executive Committee of the "Republic of Alsace-Lorraine"—René Ley, Henry Muth, and "Count" Charles Rapp—distributed pamphlets, addressed to U.S. President Warren G. Harding, affixed with postage stamps bearing the legend in English: "Alsace-Lorraine requires plebiscitum." That same year, the committee wrote the French general Auguste Hirschauer, asking "whether Prussian despotism, which for forty-seven years spit in our faces, has not been replaced by the tyranny of French imperialists. . . ." The letter concluded, "[We] demand that our Committee be allowed to speak at Strasbourg, or it will be war between France and us."[4] A later tract, written in German and dated September 1919, demanded the evacuation of Alsace by French troops and free elections under a "North American" guarantee.[5] Equally frivolous was the Alsatian party of Klaus Zorn von Bulach (younger son of the secretary of agriculture under the German Statthalter), who was described by one of his colleagues as a "madman" and as a "bad actor (*mauvais sujet*)" by the French police. Both epithets were borne out by von Bulach's wild behavior in Strasbourg cabarets and by his habit of speaking German only to his dogs and attaching his Iron Cross to their tails. In his more sober moments, Bulach demanded a "wide, regionalist regime" that would include bilingualism, equality between Alsatian and French functionaries, reduction of military service to one year, and treatment of Alsatians as first-class French citizens.[6]

However improbable, French authorities took the leaders of both organizations seriously, deporting Ley, Muth, and Rapp and keeping Bulach under surveillance.[7] Their concern was justified by the reaction that the impassioned rhetoric of these men aroused in other, more balanced Alsatian figures and organizations operating within the law. For example, the old German Zentrum had been resuscitated in April 1919 under the name Union Populaire Républicaine d'Alsace (U.P.R.). In November 1919, the party won nine of the sixteen seats allotted to Alsace in the first elections held under French rule. Then, despite a general shift to the Left reflected in the next elections (held during the spring of 1924), the party won eight of thirteen seats. The U.P.R. was committed to the preservation of local liberties and rights, recourse to the referendum on important provincial matters, and, above all, to the maintenance of the religious settlement as spelled out in the Napoleonic Concordat of 1801, in the Falloux law of 1851, and in pertinent German legislation passed between 1871 and

1881. These laws had maintained the churches, synagogues, and clergy as arms of the state and had given the religious orders wide powers over primary and secondary education. The Catholic clergy was especially influential in the U.P.R. since it was they who had taken over as the moral and intellectual leaders after 1871 when local notables and the intelligentsia, opting for French citizenship, had left the province to become exiles.

Conflict between the U.P.R. and the national government in Paris began in earnest in 1924 when the new premier, Edouard Herriot, a member of the triumphant anticlerical Cartel des Gauches (a coalition of leftists), formally announced his intention to apply an assimilationist policy in Alsace and to abolish the High Commission. Herriot justified his policy on the grounds that the French law of 1905 separating church and state had effectively abolished the Concordat in Alsace, that the Falloux law had been overturned by the Ferry anticlerical legislation passed during the 1880s, and that German laws were null and void in Alsace following the signing of the Treaty of Versailles. In response, a storm of protest swept Alsace, culminating on July 20, 1924, in a mass meeting at Strasbourg of some seventeen thousand who enthusiastically applauded denunciations of the Cartel des Gauches and the anticlerical government in Paris. (One of the orators was a U.P.R. deputy from Bas-Rhin, Michel Walter.)[8] Catholics throughout France, who were threatened by Herriot's determination to abolish the French Embassy at the Vatican and several important religious orders at home, rallied to the support of the Alsatian "clericals." In October 1924, the nation's Catholic hierarchy officially sponsored the formation of the Fédération Nationale Catholique; its leader was the "booted Capuchin" of the Battle of Verdun fame, Gen. Edouard de Curières de Castelnau, and its executive committee included Joseph Weydmann, a U.P.R. deputy from Bas-Rhin.

Although Premier Herriot abandoned his assimilationist policy in January 1925, when the Conseil d'Etat decreed that the 1801 Concordat was still valid in the three "recovered provinces," the damage had already been done. Anticlericalism from Paris had firmly and definitely pushed the U.P.R.—headed by Abbé Charles Haegy and Joseph Fasshauer (a former abbé)—into the autonomist camp. The party's daily publications, the *Elsässer* (Bas-Rhin) and the *Elsässer Kurier* (Haut-Rhin), were full of autonomist sentiment. Haegy was obsessed by the conviction that Alsace would be forced to accept the *lois laïques* ("secular laws") of the Third Republic—including separation of church and state—and was determined to use every possible means to prevent this denouement, including collaboration with the region's Communists.[9] Indeed, Alsace's Communists, headed by Charles Hueber and young Jean-Pierre Mourer (one of the autonomist leaders discussed in the next chapter), joined in demands that French authorities and troops evacuate the province and that a plebiscite be held.[10]

On May 9, 1925, there appeared in Strasbourg a new autonomist weekly, *Die Zukunft*, edited by Dr. Georges Ricklin, wartime head of the Alsatian Landtag. In 1919, Ricklin had been confined to forced residence at Kork, in the Kehl bridgehead, because his attitude was judged insufficiently patriotic by the French. Assisting Ricklin on the *Zunkunft* were René Hauss, a printer from Strasbourg; Paul Schall, a journalist and caricaturist for semipornographic publications; Auguste Hirtzel, a pastor; and Emile Pinck, a banker who was associated with an émigré German publication—of which more will be said later—the *Elsass-Lothringen Heimatstimmen*. They were a mixed bag. René Hauss's father, Charles Hauss, was a former Landtag deputy and secretary of state to the first Alsatian Statthalter during the short-lived German reform of October 1918. Schall had been condemned by the Regional Tribunal of Strasbourg for *outrages aux bonnes moeurs* ("insults to moral behavior") after the December 18, 1920, issue of one of his creations, *D'r Schliffstaan*, was seized for "representing men and women giving themselves over to the most extreme lubricity"; Schall later justified this episode with an ungrammatical pun: *"je pouvais faire de la satyr* [sic] *politique* (I certainly could become a satyr [sic] in politics)."[11]

Ricklin's *Zukunft* filled a need for the direct expression of autonomist sentiments, something the U.P.R. deputies in Paris, with their stillborn projects for regional reform, could not satisfy. By the end of 1925, one Alsatian family in twelve read the paper: this does not, of course, mean that every reader was an autonomist, but the police were already describing the publication as the head of the "anti-French movement."[12] Indeed, in late 1926 Ricklin dropped Pinck from the *Zukunft's* board of directors for being too pro-German. Denouncing separatism, Ricklin repeatedly stated that autonomy was desired only within the political framework of France.[13] Nevertheless, the official attitude toward Ricklin was very cautious: a prefectoral report at the time describes him as "very clerical, very authoritarian, using religion a great deal for the satisfaction of his political ambitions. . . ."[14]

Thus, in the few short years following the euphoria of 1918 and 1919, lay, religious, and Bolshevik versions of autonomy had emerged. And there were more to come. On June 8, 1926, a new regional organization, the Alsace-Lorraine Heimatbund published its manifesto, an "appeal to all Alsace-Lorrainers faithful to their homeland."

For seven years, we have witnessed . . . the disgusting spectacle of a methodical spoilation; on our own territory, we are deprived of our rights, we are forgotten, the solemn promises given to us are trampled in the dust, the qualities of our race and language are ignored, our traditions and customs are mocked. . . . Today . . . the fanatical partisans of assimilation intend to attack the character, soul, and even the civilization of the Alsace-Lorraine people, without any respect for the liberty of conscience. . . .

Under no pretext will we henceforth bear this misery.

We are convinced that . . . the inalienable rights of the people of Alsace-Lorraine . . . can only be guaranteed . . . by complete autonomy within the framework of France.

This legislative and administrative autonomy is naturally expressed by a representative assembly elected by our people, with budgetary powers, and by an executive power sitting at Strasbourg. The members of this latter-named [group] will be taken from the Alsace-Lorraine people and will be empowered to maintain contact with the Parliament at Paris, the only body competent [to pass on] general French problems.

We demand that Christian conviction . . . be fully respected and instead of being destroyed, it be allowed to develop freely . . . the moral forces it gives us in abundance. . . .

We forcefully demand that the German language . . . occupy in public life the place it deserves. In school . . . it will appear in the examinations. In the administration and tribunals, it will be used . . . on the same level as French. . . .

We insist that our compatriots . . . alone can free us from an archaic bureaucracy. . . . We are enthusiastic partisans of the idea of peace and international collaboration. . . .

Being on the soil where two great civilizations are in contact, our homeland should have its part in the

> construction of a common civilization of western and
> central Europe.
>   . . . We wish to group the Alsace-Lorraine people
> into a league, the "Heimatbund." . . . We will not form
> a new party, we will be only a new organization which
> will force the existing parties to renounce their hesita-
> tions, weaknesses, and errors, and will lead the battle
> for the rights and claims of the Alsace-Lorraine people
> with untiring energy.
>   Long live a strong, free, and healthy Alsace-
> Lorraine.[15]

This radical manifesto was signed by ninety-eight
men, of whom fifteen were priests or pastors; others were
doctors, teachers, railway workers, miners, local representatives, pharmacists, mayors, wine-growers, engineers,
professors, and farmers—all from Haut-Rhin, Bas-Rhin,
or Moselle. Among the signers were three who emerged
as important autonomist leaders—Jean-Pierre Mourer,
Joseph Rossé, and Marcel Stürmel—and a more anonymous group which would function as the movement's
general staff during the interwar period: Victor Antoni,
Fasshauer, Hauss, Jean Keppi, Julien Marco, Camille
Meyer, Ricklin, Karl Roos, Schall, René Schlegel, and
Abbé Joseph Zemb.[16]

Within two years, the Heimatbund began issuing
its own newspaper, the *Volkstimme* (edited first in
Saarguemines and then, from December 1926 on, in
Strasbourg). The Heimatbund also spawned two new
autonomist parties during the late 1920s: they were the
Alsatian Progressive party (Elsässische Fortschrittpar-
tei), a moderate group under the leadership of Pastor
Georges Wolf, and the separatist Landespartei, led by
Hauss, Schall, Pinck, and Karl Roos. (The Landespartei
was created by the fusion of one wing of the Heimatbund
with Zorn von Bulach's Alsatian opposition block. Von
Bulach had agreed to the merger while serving a thirteen-

month sentence incurred for threatening the life of the French prefect of Bas-Rhin.)[17] By 1928 Wolf had begun publishing yet another autonomist journal, *Das neue Elsass,* and the irrepressible Bulach, *Die Wahrheit.*

What accounts for the proliferation of autonomist activity and the profusion of the movement's publications during these early interwar years? Part of the answer lies in the refusal of Paris either to pass remedial, decentralizing legislation or to sympathize with the autonomist cause. For example, the regionalist bill of August 1926, granting limited autonomy, was never even submitted to the French Chamber of Deputies or to the Senate for debate. The visits to Alsace by premiers Paul Painlevé and Raymond Poincaré, in September 1925 and October 1926, were disastrous in terms of reconciliation with France. And when the Radical-Socialist Edouard Daladier visited in February 1929, he was kidnapped at the Saverne railway station by two autonomist students who forced him to ride around the countryside all day with them; Daladier appeared in time only for dessert at the Strasbourg banquet honoring him.[18]

Another reason, however, for heightened autonomist activity involves its backing by German interests and money; the chief conduit of both to the Alsatians was Robert Ernst. Because Ernst was so important in the history of modern Alsatian autonomism and to the movement's leaders, his background deserves some attention. Ernst was born in Hurtigheim (Bas-Rhin) on February 4, 1897, the son of an Alsatian pastor. While most of the family successfully made the transition to French rule after 1918, Robert Ernst and his parents did not: they chose to leave their homeland for the Reich in order to remain German citizens.[19] The move did not dissolve Ernst's interest in Alsace, however; at the University of Tübingen, he organized an all-German Alsatian students' league and joined an Alsatian mutual-aid society, the Hilfsbund der Elsass-Lothringer im Reich.

It is possible that Ernst may have been introduced to irredentist activity through these contacts. By 1921, the Hilfsbund der Elsass-Lothringer im Reich was already distributing throughout Germany the autonomist pamphlets of the Executive Committee of the "Republic of Alsace-Lorraine." That same year, Ernst began editing the *Elsass-Lothringen Heimatstimmen,* a deluxe monthly devoted to the affairs of the lost Reichsland. Naturally, German interest in the region was high among both private and public individuals. For example, despite a 1921 German Foreign Ministry report which described Rapp as a "swindler" and Ley as a "psychopath," their autonomist executive committee received some indirect financial support from German propaganda sources, as well as from German heavy industry and from anti-French sympathizers in Britain, the United States, and Mexico. (This backing was secret, of course, and when Ley was finally seized by the French and imprisoned in Paris in 1925, the Germans who had supported his group would have nothing to do with him.)[20] In any case, by 1923, spurred by the general climate and by his own special ties, Robert Ernst had acquired a reputation within Germany as an anti-French firebrand. In a letter dated March 6, 1923, he wrote, "We must try to strike the Frenchman wherever he is vulnerable . . . [and] make the Alsatians and Lorrainers [who have been] incorporated into the French army the carriers of the bacillus of mutiny." Such sentiments perhaps explain why the staid *Frankfurter Zeitung* did not, at the time, dare publish Ernst's articles on Alsace.[21]

Ernst profited from the general upsurge in German irredentist activity after 1924 and soon became the chief supporter of the autonomist cause across the Rhine.[22] He met Charles Hauss in Kehl in 1924 and gave him funds to help start the *Zukunft*; Ernst continued this aid to Emile Pinck after Hauss died. It seems probable that Ricklin, Fasshauer, Abbé Haegy, and Joseph Rossé (Haegy's young, bright, and ambitious protégé, who was head of the main bureaucrats' and teachers' organization in Alsace), approached Ernst for help in establishing a newspaper and, above all, in launching the Heimatbund.[23] Ernst later claimed that Charles Hauss and Georges Ricklin had pressured him into becoming involved with the autonomists, and that he had modified his irredentist aims to support a program of minority and cultural rights within France because in the meetings with Hauss, he saw the Alsatian situation for the first time as it really was.[24] In fact, however, on October 23, 1926, shortly after the Heimatbund manifesto had been issued, Ernst met with Ricklin's representative, Joseph Fasshauer, near Zürich at the Zofingen home of a Swiss sympathizer, Eugen Wildi (whom Ernst later described as the "best friend I have on earth").[25] At this meeting, Ernst gave Fasshauer 100,000 Swiss francs to establish a printing firm, the Erwinia, in Strasbourg; it immediately began publishing the *Zukunft*, the *Volkstimme*, and the *Wahrheit*. The money apparently came from private individuals, Germans with industrial connections. In this case, the sponsors included a Mr. Goetz, one of the Liberal deputies from Alsace to the Reichstag before 1918; Goetz counted the well-known steel magnate Hermann Roechling among his many industrialist friends in southwest Germany.[26]

Official German sources of funds for the autonomists were more cautious in responding to Ernst's appeals. In 1921 the German Foreign Office had refused money to the Alsace-Lorraine branch of the paramilitary Deutsche Schutzbund; but in 1924 it began to support the Alsatian autonomists by giving aid to the émigré-staffed Elsass-Lothringisches Wissenschaftliches Institut an der Universität Frankfurt-am-Main.[27] Although the Foreign Office refused Ernst's pleas for a subsidy of the *Zukunft* in April 1925, by 1927 it was giving 280,000RM annually to the autonomist cause.[28] It is worth noting that Robert Ernst and the officials of the Auswärtiges Amt spoke always of Alsace within the framework of France. But Gustav Stresemann, the foreign minister who had officially renounced Alsace-Lorraine for Germany at Locarno on March 7, 1925, privately longed for a weakening of the region's ties with France.[29]

Along with their "secular" colleagues, the "clerical" Alsatian autonomists were not neglected by the Germans. Beginning in August and September 1926, other funds were distributed through the Reverend Emile Clément Scherer to Fasshauer and to Joseph Rossé. Scherer, an Alsatian with dual citizenship, was a member of the Strasbourg diocese, secretary of the Verein des deutschen Katholiken im Ausland, a close friend of Ernst's, and a frequent visitor to Alsace.[30] He was, in short, a perfect go-between. Another of Ernst's contacts, Albert Bongartz, an Alsatian teacher, was especially influential in arranging several interviews during the late summer between the Germans and the Alsatian "clericals." These meetings were held in Switzerland, probably at Mariastein near Basel.[31] With the Zofingen and Mariastein contacts, the two major clandestine channels of communication between the Alsatian autonomists and their German supporters at last were established.

For a time during the mid-1920s, it seemed as if autonomism was spreading like wildfire. In March 1926, for example, Alsatians met in Zürich with German Rhinelanders, Swiss, and Austrians to discuss a buffer state (*état-tampon*) comprised of the four Catholic regions situated between laic France and Protestant Prussia.[32] Furthermore, there were contacts with the Breton autonomist movement—the Breiz Atao—dating from 1927, when Alsatians joined Bretons and Corsicans to form the Comité central des minorités nationales de France.[33] Even the Strasbourg Esperanto Association was taken over on November 7, 1927, by autonomists— "of bad moral character," according to a police report.[34] Autonomists encountered hostility in Alsace, however: in the middle of an uproarious meeting in August 1927, they were prevented from entering the Salle des Catherinettes in Colmar by a crowd of about four hundred "patriots including republicans, royalists, fascists, veterans, and volunteers" from all over the region. When autonomists tried to hold a subsequent meeting at the Cercle catholique Saint-Martin, it too was disrupted. During the affray, one autonomist had a "nervous seizure (*attaque de nerfs*)" and "stones and bottle shards flew through the air, a sport in which the celebrated Abbé Rohmer of Wintzenheim excelled."[35] It was this episode which prompted the autonomists to establish their own paramilitary protection force, the Schutztruppe, an action Paul Schall later defended as necessary and as no more extremist a step than the establishment of defense leagues by other political parties "except the Radical Socialists, probably because they don't have any members."[36]

Despite the movement's apparent strength, fissures soon appeared between what has been referred to as the "three autonomies"—the Catholic Haut-Rhin wing, the lay and liberal Bas-Rhin wing, and the anti-French separatist wing (concentrated along the Palatinate border). The Union Populaire Républicaine, exhibiting the first signs of a split between autonomists and the more moderate "nationalists" within its ranks, assumed an aloof and even hostile attitude toward the Heimatbund.[37] Joseph Rossé, who was so important in developing contacts with Ernst and Scherer, expressed misgivings about signing the Heimatbund manifesto and about linking the U.P.R. to its goals; in October 1927, he resigned from the Bund when it formed the new, separatist-oriented Landespartei. That same fall, the U.P.R.'s Directors' Committee rejected the Heimatbund goal of legislative autonomy as unconstitutional, proposing instead to work for Alsatian administrative autonomy.[38]

Differences began to appear within the Catholic ranks as well. In October 1926, the pro-French archbishop of Strasbourg, Monsignor Charles Ruch, condemned both the Bund and the *Zukunft*, leaving the leading autonomists to petition the Vatican for redress.[39] Late the following year, a twenty-two page protest was delivered to Pope Pius XI by Ricklin, Jean Keppi (first general secretary of the Heimatbund), and others. Following Abbé Haegy's reasoning, they claimed that a temporary alliance with the Communists and with other secular parties was necessary to save Alsace from the influence of Freemasonry (*Loge de Paris*). The petition, however, was in vain. The Vatican rejected the autonomists' argument, assuring the French government that it would send a representative to look after Haegy, someone who would have the "entire confidence of Mgr. Ruch and [would be] capable of enlightening the politician priest in [his] future conduct."[40] Haegy refused Rome's fiat and stuck to his position, asserting that "in their hearts" Catholics in Alsace, in France, and in Rome understood and supported his policy of pragmatic alliances.[41]

Official reaction against the autonomists quickly followed. Since 1926, the French government had taken reprisals against signers of the Heimatbund manifesto; Joseph Rossé, fired from his teaching post, was one of the earliest victims. Now, apparently, the national government felt broader actions were necessary. The *Zukunft*, the *Volkstimme*, and the *Wahrheit* were outlawed in November 1927. Then, during the night of December 24–25, a vast sweep of arrests was carried out all over Alsace; the choice of Christmas Eve for the police action was considered scandalous by pious Alsatians. (These raids also included the seizure of documents and personal effects of those taken into custody.) Ricklin, Hauss, Schall, Fasshauer (and his mistress, Agnès Eggemann), Rossé, Marcel Stürmel, and others—twenty-four in all—were arrested and jailed in Colmar. Roos, Ernst, Ley, Pinck, and Hirtzel had already fled to, or remained in, Switzerland and Germany.[42]

What, exactly, was the French government's case against the so-called Colmar defendants? The vast dossier usually associated with a trial of such magnitude has disappeared, lost in the hasty evacuation of June 1940; only some of the interrogatory sessions of the pretrial process (*instruction*) and the records of the public sessions remain.[43] But even from this documentation, it seems that Paris misjudged its case. First of all, the government grouped together as defendants those who were essentially federalists, such as Rossé and Stürmel, and those who were blatantly separatists, such as Ricklin and Fasshauer. Second, it accused them of subversion, but the only evidence was rumors of contacts with Germany. All of the principals—including Ricklin, the key witness—denied these contacts under oath.[44] The leaders had arranged with Ernst before their arrest that if the Erwinia loan ever came to light, Wildi, not Ernst, would assume responsibility so as "not to abandon the Alsatian autonomists."[45]

All of the defendants insisted that autonomism was meant within the political framework of France, that it did not mean separatism. This argument, so crucial to their case, was perhaps encouraged in part by one of the assistant defense counsels, a Breiz Atao militant; it was a point reiterated frequently throughout the Colmar trial. Paul Schall testified that before its fusion with von Bulach's Alsatian party, the Heimatbund had rejected a program which would have reestablished the constitution of 1911 and ordered a plebiscite to determine whether or not Alsace would remain French. Joseph Rossé, after all, had resigned from the Heimatbund when, in his view, it developed separatist tendencies. Even Ricklin expressed similar sentiments regarding the validity of the French cadre principle. After a public trial lasting twenty-four days, Hauss, Schlegel, Madame Eggemann, and Stürmel were acquitted; Rossé, Ricklin, Schall, and Fasshauer were found guilty of plotting against the security of the state, given one-year prison sentences, and prohibited from entering Alsace (*interdiction de séjour*) for five years. Those in flight were given heavy sentences: Ley, twenty years in prison; Roos, Pinck, and Ernst, fifteen.[46]

Despite these convictions, the autonomists were definitely exculpated in Alsatian opinion. This sentiment had been demonstrated in the spring elections of 1928: eleven autonomist deputies (from a total of sixteen) had been returned to the parliament in Paris, including two imprisoned in Colmar—Ricklin and Rossé. When the Chamber of Deputies voted 195 to 29, with 350 abstentions, not to seat Ricklin and Rossé, the mood was confirmed in the post-trial by-elections: autonomists Marcel Stürmel and René Hauss were triumphantly chosen to fill the seats.[47] By the end of 1928, both Ricklin and Rossé had been released from official custody, although Rossé was still prohibited from entering Alsace for five years and deprived of his civil rights. This sentence was lifted by an undated amnesty sometime before Rossé became a candidate for municipal councillor of Colmar in October 1930.[48] Within eighteen months, the judgment in absentia against Karl Roos, one of the most militant anti-French leaders of the Landespartei, had been overturned by the Supreme Court of Appeals (Cour de cassation) sitting at Besançon.[49] Then, in January 1931, a general amnesty was declared for all those charged at Colmar in 1928.

It seemed at this point that Fasshauer's statement at Colmar was being borne out: "If I am an autonomist, that is my right just as it is to be [a] royalist." But the strength of the movement remained to be tested. Would the future fulfill the program issued in January 1928 by Roos and others exiled in Basel? This second manifesto demanded not only legislative and administrative autonomy for Alsace, but also "protection" of Alsatian mores, customs, and privileges and "cultivation" of the German language that "for one thousand five hundred years has been the mother tongue of one and one-half million Alsace-Lorrainers."[50]

The answer is that the autonomists' program was not fulfilled by the French and was, in fact, utterly destroyed by the German occupation of Alsace from 1940 to 1944–45. The road to this denouement, the total capitulation of the autonomists, and to the bitter French reprisals against them after World War II, was a long and tortuous one. It began with the first elections after the shock of the Colmar trial had begun to abate. As a result of these municipal elections, held during May 1929, a Communist, Charles Hueber, became mayor of Alsace's capital, Strasbourg. Hueber's victory was due not only to his heavy autonomist and Communist support in the city, but also to the U.P.R.'s backing: Michel Walter, a U.P.R. leader, was named vice-mayor.

The election of Hueber and Walter had two curious

repercussions. First, Hueber was excluded from the official French Communist party for having collaborated with bourgeois forces. This was strange since the party vehemently favored Alsatian autonomy; in fact, the Communist leader, Maurice Thorez, proclaimed at the time, "*We support the right of freedom of choice for the people of Alsace-Lorraine up to and including separation from France.*" The other effect was the victory several months later of a nationalist splinter group of the U.P.R. in a complementary senatorial election held in Ribeau-villé (Haut-Rhin).[51] Dr. Joseph Pfleger, one of the leaders of the Action populaire nationale d'Alsace (A.P.N.A.) since its founding in Strasbourg in November 1928, defeated the formidable autonomist, Abbé Charles Haegy of the *Elsässer Kurier.* Pfleger's success indicated that the new A.P.N.A., although bereft of the U.P.R.'s popular and clerical support, was a force to be reckoned with.

The original autonomist Heimatfront (or, as it came to be called after the Colmar trial, Volksfront) had extremely varied electoral success during the early 1930s. It failed to elect Rossé as a municipal councillor in Colmar in October 1930, but did succeed in naming Karl Roos a departmental councillor (*conseiller général*) in the cantonal elections a year later. In the national elections of April 1932, the Volksfront scored a seemingly great victory, with the U.P.R. retaining its five seats in Haut-Rhin and adding one to its three in Bas-Rhin. The Progressive party and new Workers' and Peasants' party (Arbeiter- und Bauernpartei)—the Communist Autonomists—also retained their Saverne and Strasbourg seats. Neither Paul Schall nor Karl Roos, however, was elected. Overall, the distribution of seats in the French Chamber of Deputies in 1932 was almost exactly that of 1928: the historian François Dreyfus has rightly termed this national election the "failure of the autonomist campaign born in 1924."[52]

A nationalist, pro-French reaction against the excesses of autonomism must be ruled out as an explanation for this failure. Nor does the lingering prosperity of the Alsatian economy as compared with the German, which was reeling under the hammer blows of the Great Depression, provide the answer. (The German Foreign Office, in fact, was forced to reduce its subsidy to the Alsatian autonomists from 280,000RM for 1928–29 to 160,000RM for 1930–31, despite the Wilhelmstrasse's fears that the movement might collapse completely without German funds.)[53] The real explanation for the electoral failure is the existence of several different wings ("autonomies") within the autonomist movement. The essentially Catholic and Haut-Rhin movement of the U.P.R. was dedicated to administrative autonomy and to the preservation of the Concordat and educational privileges given the religious orders during the nineteenth century. (Indeed, its northern branch, under the control of Strasbourg's vice-mayor, Michel Walter, was pro-French and regionalist, rather than autonomist, in outlook.) In the Progressive party (now under the leadership of Camille Dahlet, a former Radical-Socialist) the emphasis was secular, defending the native language and culture within France's political framework. Finally, in the Landespartei (led by Roos, Hauss, and Schall) and also among the Communist Autonomists (led by Hueber and Mourer)—both strong in the northern Lutheran communes, where the dialect is interchangeable with the German spoken in the Palatinate, and in the Strasbourg suburbs—the secular issues were combined with a pronounced desire for legislative autonomy and even for separatism.

These differences did not mean that the autonomist front was now hollow. Indeed, Rossé, who was elected from Colmar to the French Chamber of Deputies in May 1932, seemed at times to abandon the principle of a culturally unique Alsace within the French political framework. So too did Marcel Stürmel, the new occupant of Ricklin's seat in Paris. Furthermore, the Progressives, Communist Autonomists, and members of the Landespartei collaborated in many electoral campaigns. For example, in 1930 the three parties drew up a joint resolution urging an "energetic battle for the liberties of the people of Alsace-Lorraine." It proclaimed, "Above all, the rights of linguistic and cultural minorities . . . can very well be achieved . . . by autonomy . . . [that will in turn] defend successfully the Alsace-Lorraine *Volkstum* [national characteristics]."[54] The crucial point here is that at no time did the autonomists in Alsace form a monolithic organization of conspirators against the French state: the divergences between the various groups were too significant. An illustration of these differences occurred in June 1934, when the interdepartmental committee of the U.P.R. rejected Roos's proposition for a close alliance of all autonomist parties. The committee maintained that the U.P.R. stood, above all, for the defense of "religious interests" within the "framework of general French politics."[55]

It is probably correct to assume, as the historian Dreyfus does, that during the interwar years the vast majority of Alsatians were regionalists. While they sympathized with the autonomist aims of Rossé, Stürmel, Abbé Haegy, and Dahlet, they definitely were not separatists. Most Alsatians associated themselves with the separatists only when the "systematic lack of understanding" of regionalism by French politicians of both the Right and the Left pushed them into it. The Heimatfront and, later, the Volksfront are two clear examples of this very uneasy alliance in defense of Alsatian "rights." An illustration of this mistrust of the Alsatians by those "of the interior" was a statement by the chief prosecutor at the Colmar trial. He asserted that "under the cover of

Alsatian particularism, [Ricklin] pursues the aim of separating Alsace from France," and warned, "Do not forget that Germany is a federal state while France is one and indivisible."[56]

And yet, there were several clear examples of how regionalism and the unitary state could, in fact, be synthesized. The proposed legislation of the 1920s has already been mentioned; other similar bills were introduced, most notably in July 1931 and June 1934.[57] A lengthy report drawn up in 1935 by an Alsatian royalist leader condemned both political autonomy and separatism, but spelled out in great detail how regionalism and decentralization, its corollary, would solve the problem. In a Gallic version of the 1911 constitution, the report proposed an independent governor (*intendant*) overseeing a prefect in Strasbourg who would, in turn, be responsible for decentralized administrative services. There would also be a Consultative Council of thirty members and a Provincial Council of thirty-three members, most of whom would be elected by universal suffrage. The Consultative Council, to which the regional government would be responsible, would be consulted on all legislative measures and would be supervised by the Conseil d'Etat in Paris. In addition, the various regional administrative bureaus would have direct links to the capital; and the prefect, although independent from central control, could be removed from office within thirty days over a specific action or point of policy. The royalist report concluded by affirming that if regional decentralization were adopted for Alsace, then an all-out effort could be made to pursue the separatists—specifically, by reviving the pre-1918 German laws against high treason and lese majesty. Alsatian identity could thus be preserved within the French state, and Strasbourg could become the meeting place where "Germanism and Romanism" would be reconciled.[58]

The royalists were much more understanding of
Alsatian needs than either the *patriotard* ("jingoist")
Right or the Jacobin Left. The Alsatian Comte Jean de
Pange went to the royalist Marshal Hubert Lyautey, of
Morrocan fame, the day after the Colmar trial verdict
was handed down to ask him to become high commissioner in Alsace. The marshal, who could hardly be
suspected of tepid patriotism, replied that he "would try
to represent France in a dignified manner. I would go
on Sunday to mass with my staff . . . German would
be spoken around me."[59] But the central royalist organization, the Action Française of Charles Maurras, was the
"only political grouping [in France] which considered
the Alsatian malaise to be a political problem." The
Fédération Nationale Catholique, founded during the
anticlerical crisis of the mid-1920s, was not an organized
political party with representation in the Chamber of
Deputies; in fact, it had lost its raison d'etre with
the defeat of Herriot's measures.[60] Furthermore, the
French Communist party, which had supported autonomism until Stalin's turn toward collaboration with
France in 1934, was distinctly a minority party. And
because the parliamentary bills, as well as the royalist
report, concerned changes only for Alsace and not any
reorganization of French government as a whole, their
failure was certain: passage would have increased rather
than mitigated the province's special qualities within the
unitary French state.

This was not only a perplexing dilemma but also a
great misfortune from the French point of view because
a magnificent opportunity had arisen after January 1933
to split permanently the U.P.R. and the Progressives from
the Landespartei and the Communist Autonomists, thus
destroying the old Heimatbund. The advent of Hitler in
Germany, with his anti-religious policies and terrorist tactics, frightened the U.P.R. and the Progressives; they be-

gan to moderate their position, thus isolating the separatist members of the Landespartei and the Communist Autonomists in a kind of political ghetto. On September 21, 1933, the U.P.R. withdrew its support of Karl Roos as vice-president of the *conseil général.* This move was taken despite the Concordat between the Vatican and Hitler's government and despite the threat of what seemed to be a new anticlerical measure—the so-called Guy la Chambre circular, which would simplify the procedure for obtaining dispensations from religious instruction in the schools.[61] In the cantonal elections the following fall (October 1934), the U.P.R. and Progressives ran independently of the Landespartei. Surely its new paramilitary youth-group, the Jungmannschaft, led by a young Strasbourg lawyer, Hermann Bickler, was particularly worrisome; the Landespartei increasingly appeared to be an offshoot of National Socialism. Because of this split, autonomists were the losers in this election; even Rossé failed to gain his council seat in Colmar, despite the fact that the U.P.R. emerged as the region's strongest party. Several months later, in May 1935, autonomists also lost their majority on the Strasbourg city council. Following a rapprochement with the French government, the moderate U.P.R. was again the largest winner in the legislative elections of May 1936, holding four of nine seats in Bas-Rhin and five of seven in Haut-Rhin.[62]

Despite this victory of the moderates, and despite the fact that socio-economic issues assumed an increasing importance in the elections of the mid-1930s, autonomism was not dead: Mourer and Hueber were elected from Bas-Rhin; the Landespartei (as we shall see) was still very much alive; and questions of the place of religion, the German language, and administrative particularism were still very important. Indeed, twelve Alsatian and four Moselle deputies joined together in the new legislature in Paris to form the Groupe indépendante d'action populaire—a new, if somewhat less formidable, version of the Heimatfront. Among the Alsatian deputies were Rossé, Stürmel, Dahlet, Mourer, and Hueber.[63] A repetition of the 1924 protests against anticlerical government seemed to be in the making with the 1936 passage of a decree by the Blum government extending the obligatory schooling age in Alsace-Lorraine to fifteen years; the purpose was to achieve a "deeper knowledge of the national language." Alsatians quickly mounted protests against this measure; they feared, above all, a lessening of German language training and of religious education. Rossé filled the *Elsässer Kurier* with invectives against the atheists in the capital; U.P.R. deputy Michel Walter, at a meeting of deputies from the three departments, issued an appeal to the French people "against this government which is not France."[64] Under pressure, Paris deferred the application of the decree; eventually, in December 1937, the Conseil d'Etat overturned it as the Popular Front era was drawing to a close.

By this time, Europe was covered by the advancing shadow of war. As the Communist Autonomists, the Landespartei, and the Jungmannschaft grew closer together, the thicker their police dossiers became. Following a series of confiscations in late 1938 and the arrest of Karl Roos on February 3, 1939, French authorities unleashed a second roundup of autonomists with the declaration of war against Germany. Within ten days after September 1, 1939, fifteen of the movement's leaders were arrested and brought to the main prison at Nancy to await interrogation and trial on charges of having relations (*intelligences*) with the enemy.[65] Who were these autonomist leaders who had risen to prominence with the movement, especially since the Colmar trial? And what had German influence been upon them? The degree of this influence, varying from group to group and from man to man, would determine each one's fate during the Nazi occupation of Alsace and at the hands of the French after the Second World War.

3

The Autonomist Leaders,
1919 - 1939

Inheriting the mantle of Ricklin, Charles Hauss,
Pinck, Hirtzel, and Wolf, a handful of important autonomist leaders appeared during the tumultuous years of
the 1920s. Joseph Rossé, Marcel Stürmel, Jean-Pierre
Mourer, Armand (Hermann) Bickler, and Friedrich
Spieser dominated the politics of Alsace from the time
of the Heimatbund manifesto and the Colmar trial to
the outbreak of World War II. During this period, they
were never outshone by "nationalist" deputies to their
Right nor outflanked on the radical-racist Left by rivals
who espoused immediate return to Germany. (Camille
Dahlet, the former Radical-Socialist who succeeded
Georges Wolf as head of the Alsatian Progressive party
in 1928, has been omitted from this discussion. His party
was a minor one in the autonomist movement; his autonomism, secular in nature, was firmly planted within the
French framework; and he never had dealings with
either Weimar or Hitlerian Germany.)

First and foremost among the autonomist leaders
was Joseph Rossé, in many ways the most fascinating yet
ambiguous member of the group. Rossé led the U.P.R.'s
most important faction, that of Haut-Rhin, and was
twice elected to the French Chamber of Deputies. He
was described by Robert Wagner, Gauleiter of Baden-
Alsace during the German wartime occupation as a

"good German but not a Nazi." Perhaps the most perceptive characterization was made by Albert Bongartz, an Alsatian teacher and one of the contacts between Robert Ernst and the autonomists: after the end of the Second World War, Bongartz noted, "Rossé always landed on his feet."[1]

Born August 26, 1892, at Montreux-le-Vieux (Haut-Rhin) on the old 1871 frontier, Rossé's father was a baker who went bankrupt in 1908. Rossé was educated first in his village and then in Colmar, where he received a scholarship from the German government. In 1913 the Colmar school officials assigned Rossé to his birthplace as an assistant teacher; he was to teach his students "assimilationist" principles. Rossé fled Montreux in August 1914, when it was occupied by the French. Rejected by the German army because of poor health, he returned to his teaching training at Colmar, again with subsidies from the government. He was finally inducted into the army in November 1916 and was sent to the Russian front; there he became an officer on July 20, 1918.

After the armistice, Rossé returned to Alsace and was named as a grammar school teacher (*Mittelschullehrer*) on December 13, 1918. (Unaccountably, the selecting panel still consisted of three Germans and one Alsatian.) Rossé was sent to Lauterbourg in northern Alsace, where his anti-French attitude brought him threats of disciplinary action. Instead, however, due to his close connections with the powerful Abbé Charles Haegy, Rossé was merely sent back to the Ecole Normale at Colmar. In 1920, he took part in the general strike of Alsatian teachers and bureaucrats protesting assimilation by France. As secretary of the Fédération des fonctionnaires d'Etat et des instituteurs d'Alsace—the region's most important civil service organization—Rossé signed the Heimatbund manifesto.

Rossé's political activity soon took its toll: although

triumphantly reelected to his secretaryship—winning 146 of 149 votes in the Directors' Committee—he was dismissed from the teaching profession by the French government on August 4, 1926. (He retained, however, 90 percent of his regular pension.)[2] Rossé met in Switzerland with the Reverend Scherer in August 1926; he was arrested on Christmas Eve 1927 by French authorities in the roundup of autonomist leaders and was a defendant in the Colmar trial. While in prison, Rossé was elected to the Chamber of Deputies but was not seated. Although convicted at Colmar on charges of plotting against the security of the state, he was pardoned on July 13, 1928.

As a deputy stripped of his mandate by the Chamber, Rossé concentrated his very considerable energies on running Alsatia, Abbé Haegy's vast publishing enterprise which turned out twelve daily, weekly, and monthly publications. Following Haegy's death in 1932 Rossé became editor of the powerful *Elsässer Kurier,* after failing to secure control of the U.P.R. Bas-Rhin newspaper, the *Elsässer.* In 1936, he acquired the *Elsässer Bote,* journal of the rival nationalist group, the A.P.N.A., in a daring coup that had his enemies completely outwitted.[3] (The coup was performed with the connivance of Georges Mandel, then secretary of state for Alsatian affairs, whom Rossé had gotten to know while serving in the French Chamber of Deputies since his election in April 1932. Mandel, apparently, was trying to moderate, or "nationalize," the U.P.R. by collaborating with it at the expense of the declining A.P.N.A. In his extremely acerbic account of the incident, however, the erstwhile editor of the *Elsässer Bote,* Charles Haenggi, cited Mandel's venality as the motivation.)[4] By the late 1930s, Rossé's publishing empire was worth 20 million (1938) French francs.

Although important in a political party that, as we

have seen, took an unfriendly view of the separatist wing
of the autonomist movement, Rossé apparently had
close links with such men as Karl Roos and the young,
dynamic Alsatian neo-führer, Hermann (Armand) Bickler. For example, in 1931, Rossé founded a youth group,
the Jeunesses de l'U.P.R., modeled after Bickler's Jungmannschaft. Clad in gray shirts and black ties, the Jeunesses saluted a red and white Alsatian flag with the
cross of Lorraine on it and shouted "Vive Rossé (Rossé
lives)!" The group supported maintenance of the local
dialect and Alsatian customs and opposed "assimilation."
Although youth movements were by no means an indication of fascistic tendencies in France during the 1930s,
they were easily assimilated by the Nazis. (When Rossé
returned from imprisonment in Nancy to German Alsace
in July 1940, the *choeur de diction* ("recitation group")
of his Jeunesses was allowed to greet their leader—but
without uniforms and with "Vive l'Allemagne" added
to their salute.)[5]

From 1930 on, Rossé was against construction of
the Maginot Line; at the end of 1932 Rossé called in the
pages of the *Kurier* for the demilitarization of Alsace;
and he opposed the two-year military service law passed
by the French Chamber in March 1935 to answer Hitler's
conscription of German males. That same year, after the
Saar voted to rejoin Germany, Rossé urged a plebiscite
in Alsace, pointing to Ireland as an example of liberation
from alien control. He supported the German view of
the 1938 Sudeten crisis which led up to France's capitulation at Munich: the whole matter was a "British affair"
according to Rossé.[6] His speeches delivered in Alsace, in
contrast with those he delivered in the Chamber in Paris,
were inflammatory: at one cantonal meeting of U.P.R.
delegates on March 25, 1934, he called for administrative
autonomy with an Alsatian Landtag. In themselves,
these sentiments were not out of keeping with Rossé's

interpretation of U.P.R. policy, but this time he added that France was "rotten," governed by "bums *(voyous)* like Guy La Chambre," and was unable to renew itself through a feeble old man, Premier Gaston Doumergue. But apparently his tough line was not persuasive. A few months later, in June 1934, Rossé was unable to force the interdepartmental committee of the U.P.R. to accept collaboration with Karl Roos and the Landespartei, despite his (Rossé's) pleas that they should collaborate with all parties which had as an aim the "defense of the province's rights."[7]

Rossé's presence at the two congresses of German-speaking Catholics, held at Freiburg-im-Breisgau during August and September 1929 and 1937, was well advertised and was taken as a sign of his continuing contacts with German friends.[8] (Rossé defended his attendance at the 1937 congress as part of his normal duties as a journalist and as *rapporteur* ["editor of reports"] of the Commission des Finances of the French Chamber—a curious role indeed for a member of the commission!)[9] Rossé never broke these German links. Beginning with his mission to Ernst before the publication of the Heimatbund manifesto in 1925 and his interviews with the Reverend Scherer in August and September 1926, Rossé maintained direct ties with his German contacts throughout the interwar period—not only with the "clericals," but also with Ernst. The letters of Albert Bongartz are eloquent testimony to these connections: in one, Rossé was given Ernst's instructions for actions to be taken during the 1928 electoral campaign in Alsace. Bongartz even claimed that Rossé received money from Ernst, but at Rossé's postwar trial, Bongartz was unable to furnish any proof.[10]

The source of most of Rossé's funds seems to have been the "clericals"—Scherer and his Catholic German colleagues—drawn, initially at least, from the Zentrum.[11]

Rossé's chauffeur testified in 1939 and 1940 at the Nancy trial that he drove his master to Germany twelve times a year, most often to Freiburg-im-Breisgau. But the chauffeur knew none of the details. Rossé always had himself left alone at a given location, returned there alone, and never "confided" the purpose of these visits or the names of those whom he saw to his chauffeur, who spent the intervening time in Freiburg's cinema.[12] The money transactions, however, which were crucial, apparently took place at Mariastein near Basel, with Rossé and Scherer in attendance. Their meeting of November 1 and 2, 1938, was especially important. When Ernst's "dearest friend" Eugen Wildi (of the Erwinia loan affair) and Bongartz, Ernst's contact-man, were arrested in Switzerland, Ernst, Roos, and Jean-Pierre Mourer fled the country, thus breaking up a meeting arranged for October 27, 1938. So on November 1 Rossé and Scherer met alone; and they spent that night burning incriminating documents. Rossé received funds from Scherer for himself and for Abbé Joseph Brauner, director of the Strasbourg Municipal Archives.[13]

Rossé later admitted that this meeting with Scherer had taken place, but argued that it was only to arrange the renewal of the latter's French passport—certainly a strange time and place for such a transaction.[14] Moreover, Scherer was at the time a refugee from the Gestapo which, with the administrative muddle-headedness typical of Nazi Germany, was determined to stop the flow of ecclesiastical revenues to the Alsatian autonomists. After the meeting, Rossé got back to Colmar, but Scherer was arrested by the Swiss authorities on November 8, 1938. He was released but was rearrested on January 10, 1939. After being freed in March 1939, Scherer fled to Brazil (via Rome), apparently taking with him some of the funds of his Verein des deutschen Katholiken im Ausland. From Brazil, Scherer wrote the German Foreign Office in July 1940, after the victory over France, saying that he wished to return to his homeland (*Heimat*) and collaborate with Rossé, "a German patriot in the best sense of the word."[15] Scherer also wanted the extensive French police dossiers on him, drawn up by the indefatigable inspector Antoine Becker, to be destroyed. Scherer's plea went unanswered by the Germans; his French files disappeared into the "interior" and were never found. (Antoine Becker, however, charged with the pursuit of the autonomists by the Sûreté Nationale, was not as fortunate as the cleric in far-off Brazil. Becker, who had become a police commissioner in Marseilles after the fall of France, was seized by the Germans in 1943 after having been denounced by someone named Basy, a figure connected to both Bongartz and Jean-Pierre Mourer. Becker was brought to Alsace and shot near the concentration camp of Natzwiller later in the year.)[16]

The November 1938 meeting at Mariastein was the single most important instance of collusion between Rossé and German agents. Indeed, Rossé was the most careful of all the autonomist leaders in his dealings with the Germans. For example, two months after the Mariastein meeting, Rossé stayed away from a meeting in Paris at the Gare d'Orsay between Ernst's courier, Gustaf Fineman (a Swedish concert tour organizer who was to have paid the autonomists in Dutch gulden), and Karl Roos, Jean-Pierre Mourer, Paul Schall, and René Hauss; Rossé's absence was "because of his prudence," in Roos's disillusioned words.[17] Rossé also spurned invitations to two other dangerous conclaves, one on February 10, 1939, in Frankfurt-am-Main, the other in Paris during April 1939.[18] He was particularly careful to cover his tracks: he claimed that early in 1939, when he "discovered" Scherer's subsidy of three periodicals printed by the Alsatia corporation, he ordered their publication to cease. The real reason, however, was not outraged patriotism but Rossé's realization that to continue receiving subsidies from Scherer had become too dangerous. During his later trials, Rossé referred to his "spontaneous and solemn" denunciation of reopening the "Alsace-Lorraine case" when rumors to this effect began circulating in Paris after the Munich agreements.[19]

A contemporary police report on Rossé was quite accurate in describing him as supple, clever, and able to convert personal attacks into an "oppression of the Alsatian consciousness"; the report advised "very great prudence" in his surveillance by the authorities. As a fellow Colmarien later said of him, "Rossé pursued simultaneously two different political strategies: one, in Alsace, where he was the champion of complaints which went as far as separation from France; the other, in Paris, where he succeeded in establishing a reputation as a mere deputy of the opposition."[20] And, as will be seen, Rossé would again succeed in his tightrope-walking efforts during the Nazi occupation of Alsace. Up to the liberation in 1945, he literally defied attempts by both the French and the Germans to find him guilty of illegal acts. Glib, elusive, and sly, Rossé had the best of both worlds for over twenty years until the Gestapo and the *épuration* ("purge") descended upon him at the close of the Second World War.

Marcel René Stürmel was Rossé's colleague in the U.P.R. and in the Chamber of Deputies in Paris. Both were known as the most autonomist-oriented of their party's leaders; both were deputies; both had similar careers; and yet Stürmel's power—between the wars and during the German occupation of Alsace from 1940 to 1945—was never as great as Rossé's. The region's mixed alliances were reflected in Stürmel's family. He was born in 1900 in Brunstaat (Haut-Rhin), the son of an ardent

Francophile who had served two seven-year hitches in the French army although officially a German subject. Stürmel's mother, a German, was his father's second wife; a half-brother from the first marriage left Alsace before 1914 as a *réfractaire* ("draft evader"), volunteered for the French army, and fought at Verdun.[21] For this reason, the elder Stürmel was deported to Biberach in Württemberg in December 1914, placed under German police surveillance, and was not allowed to return to Brunstaat until the following April. Marcel Stürmel was mobilized into the German army in June 1918 and, from the armistice of that year until 1920, was employed in the administrative services of the French national railroads. He then fulfilled his military service in the French army with the class of 1920 and in a railway unit at Versailles, where he remained until June 1921.[22]

Stürmel returned to Mulhouse in 1921, where he continued as a railroad worker and became active in the industry's unions and in the new U.P.R. Before long, he was a cherished protégé of both Ricklin's and Abbé Haegy's. He was number ninety on the list of the signers of the 1926 Heimatbund manifesto, became a member of the Bund's central committee, and established a Bund section in Mulhouse. Stürmel, allegedly, was the one who obtained weapons for the Bund at the time of the fracas in Colmar with the "patriots."[23] Dismissed from his job because of his political activities, Stürmel suffered the indignity of having his house raided by the French police on Christmas Eve 1927, but he himself was not arrested until February 24, 1928. He was acquitted by the Colmar trial jury and soon was elected departmental councillor (*conseiller général*) of the canton of Saint-Amarin (Haut-Rhin).[24] In the 1929 special election, Stürmel was triumphantly chosen by the voters of Altkirch (Haut-Rhin), his new home town, to replace the "lion of the Sundgau"—Ricklin—who, after his ex-

perience at Colmar, was too disgusted with, and indeed
too frightened by, political life to run again.

In Paris, Stürmel fought vigorously for amnesty for
those condemned at Colmar[25] and developed into something of an expert on agricultural, social, and corporate
questions. He was especially influenced by Joseph Bilger, later head of the Union paysanne d'Alsace, in these
new fields of specialization.[26] Stürmel also took a leading
part in the annual debates over the budget for the Services d'Alsace et de Lorraine.[27] In 1937, the Blum government in Paris brought him to trial in Mulhouse for false
representation of claims of war damages; Stürmel maintained that the charges were an attempt to rob him of
his decisive electoral victory in May 1936. He was found
innocent of the charges at his trial and then won the
prosecution's appeal in the Colmar courts.[28] But Stürmel
had still another legal case on his mind: at about the
same time, he sued the author of a Mulhouse lampoon
in which "Stürmel" was made to rhyme with "Dürmel,"
a word in Alsatian dialect meaning "imbecile" and
"stupid." Apparently, ridicule of this sort was too much
even for the disabused politicians of the waning Third
Republic.[29]

During the period between his dismissal from his
railway job in 1926 and his election as deputy from
Altkirch in 1929, an era he later described as the "most
dangerous and hard[est] of my life," Stürmel turned his
hand to writing articles for the *Zukunft*, the *Volkstimme*,
and the *Elsässer Kurier*.[30] He became the editor of a
monthly periodical published by Alsatia, the *Heimat*,
which had a wide following among the clergy and
Catholic teachers of Haut-Rhin. Thus, he too came in
contact with Reverend Emile Clément Scherer; according to a contemporary police report, it was Scherer who
had "negotiated" Stürmel's running for office in Ricklin's
place in 1929.[31] Through Scherer and Abbé Joseph

Brauner, Stürmel received German funds for the *Heimat* and made trips to Mariastein, sometimes with Rossé, to obtain the money from the movement's German friends.[32] Although Stürmel denied that monetary transactions took place during the Mariastein meetings, the French police viewed his journal as a vehicle for promoting the "German spirit" and autonomism among its unsuspecting readers. They regarded Stürmel himself as a social climber "devoured by ambition" and "suspect from the national point of view."[33] During his term as French secretary of state for Alsace-Lorraine affairs, a cynical Camille Chautemps said of Stürmel, "He has received only six thousand francs. So little! If we imprisoned all journalists who have received money from Germany, we would never be finished with the problem!"[34] But Stürmel was more than a mere journalist; he was the deputy for Altkirch as well. In retrospect, it was all too convenient for him to view his actions as natural and noble: "Paris wouldn't listen to us, so we turned to the Germans." The truth is that simple greed for German money—both the funds just described and those sought during the Nazi occupation as compensation for having precipitated the "national revolution" in Alsace—would prove to be Stürmel's undoing.[35]

From the point of view of the French police, Jean-Pierre Mourer was the most detested of the autonomist leaders: at his arraignment in 1946 as the former Kreisleiter of Mulhouse, his morals were described as "doubtful," his reputation, "bad," and his character, "choleric and brutal."[36] And yet Mourer had served for twelve years as head of an authentic Communist autonomist party, centered in the Strasbourg suburbs, and had been elected by his district three times to the Chamber of Deputies in Paris. In studying Mourer, we begin to move

out of the relatively settled realm of "clerical" autonomism into the jungle of "secular" autonomism in Bas-
Rhin, where a personality like Mourer's could flourish.

Mourer was born on August 19, 1897, in Wittring,
near Saarguemines (Moselle), the son of Nicolas
Chrétien Mourer and Marie Catherine (née Schoeser);
his father was the local station-master. Jean-Pierre was
educated at Wittring before attending institutions of
higher learning in Saarguemines, Montigny-les-Metz,
and Saarebourg. He served in the German army during
World War I, first in Volhynia, then in France. After
the armistice, he was employed by the Coal Reparations
Board and then by the French national railways. Mourer
was dismissed from the latter job because of his part in
a strike; nevertheless, he became secretary of the Union
des syndicats des cheminots d'Alsace-Lorraine and
steered it into the French Confédération Générale du
Travail in 1923.[37] That year, while he was giving a
speech in Frankfurt against the French occupation of
the Ruhr, Mourer met Ernst for the first time. Mourer
signed the Heimatbund manifesto in 1926 and in 1928
was elected a Communist deputy (Strasbourg Ouest and
Sud); his second ballot victory came with the aid of the
U.P.R. and the Landespartei. He was not involved in the
Colmar trial, although he reproached the government for
prosecuting the "little fry [lampistes] and not the
tenors."[38]

Like his associate, Charles Hueber, Mourer was
excluded from the national Communist party in 1930 for
his electoral alliances with "clericals"; shortly thereafter,
he founded the Alsatian Workers' and Peasants' party
(Elsässische Arbeiter- und Bauernpartei, referred to in
this work as the Communist Autonomists). Sitting not
with the Communists in the Chamber of Deputies, but
first with the Left Independent Republicans and then
with the autonomist Groupe indépendant d'action popu-

laire, Mourer became a member of the Commission for
Alsace-Lorraine, the Commission of Public Works, and
the Commission for Colonies. Several months after
testifying as a defense witness in the 1939 trial of Karl
Roos, Mourer fled to Luxembourg with associates from
the Landespartei. Returning to Paris when the Chambers
were convened in August 1939, he then retired to Périgueux, where the bulk of the Strasbourg population had
been evacuated. On October 28, 1939, Mourer was
arrested and brought to the prison in Nancy to face
French charges of treason, along with the other leading
autonomist figures.[39]

Mourer's activities with his party—he was in charge
of the German-speaking minor functionaries, petit bourgeois, and artisans, while Hueber was in charge of the
workers—brought him into close contact with the Landespartei and thus with Karl Roos, Paul Schall, René
Hauss, and ultimately with Robert Ernst himself. During
the Nazi occupation of Alsace, Mourer described himself
as an "intimate collaborator (*Intimer Mitarbeiter*)" of
the "martyred" Roos.[40] This was a somewhat curious
statement when one realizes that Roos, during the winter
of 1939–40 at Nancy, in attempting to escape execution
by a French firing squad, had put the blame for his
espionage on Mourer. (Roos's reasoning, according to
his own testimony shortly before his death, was that
Mourer, as a French deputy, would run less risk than
he would and that when the danger of sentencing was
over, he could deny his declarations to the authorities.)[41]
Mourer's description is curious too in that he always
viewed his association with Roos as an expedient. Mourer later testified that "politically formed in the breast of
the [Communist] Party, I learned that [one] must support an adverse movement when there was a partial or
passing community of interests."[42]

The Landespartei was deeply and permanently

divided by the conflicting interests of its leaders—Roos, Schall, and Hauss—and by the intruding presence of a new, young dynamic separatist who modeled himself after Hitler, Hermann (Armand) Bickler. Under these conditions, it is not surprising that the chief source of German funds to the "secular" autonomists, Robert Ernst, eventually turned to Mourer as a pacifier and as the primary distributor of money among the quarreling Landespartei leaders. Mourer's selection occurred toward the end of 1937, after both Schall and Roos had been tested in the position and found wanting. Schall, Ernst's favorite between 1928 and 1931, had cheated Ernst over the real number of copies printed of the party's newspaper, the *E.L.Z.* (*Elsass-Lothringische Zeitung*). Roos, Ernst's subsequent choice for the position from 1931 to 1933, became deeply emboiled in a public divorce scandal, a complication that Ernst, as a faithful family man and the son of a pastor, could not overlook.[43] (The source for this inside information was Julien Marco, Roos's chauffeur and secretary of the Landespartei. He was kept on during Roos's tenure, although others, including Mourer, regarded him as a "dangerous madman" because he knew too much about his employer's private life.[44] Marco's testimony given at Nancy in 1939 and 1940 provided key evidence against Roos, detailing his relations with Germany. When the Nancy prisoners were liberated by the Germans in July 1940, Marco was the only one not allowed to return to Alsace. He was deported to Germany and was later murdered at the concentration camp of Mauthausen.)

In his capacity as chief contact with the autonomists, Mourer met twenty times with Bongartz, Ernst's contact-man, and six or seven times with Ernst himself at Freiburg-im-Breisgau, in Cologne, and in Switzerland. Mourer was to have attended the famous meeting of October 27, 1938, broken up by the arrests of Wildi and

Bongartz. Mourer later disingenuously maintained that if his sudden departure from Basel at the time "resembled flight, it is because it is never good for a politician to be linked to a foreign affair."[45]

Mourer seems to have been greatly concerned with reestablishing Roos both in Ernst's favor and as a dominant force in the Landespartei. Mourer made trips to Switzerland and to see Bongartz on Roos's behalf and attended the Gare d'Orsay meeting in January 1939 to ensure that Schall did not try to undermine Roos. Indeed, there was a strong and self-interested motive for Mourer to espouse Roos's cause against the "do-nothing" Hauss, the "ineffectual" Schall, and the "petty lawyer" Bickler.[46] It can be found in Mourer's well-justified suspicion that Roos would be the first to be arrested by the French police; thus, in the projected fusion between his own Communist Autonomist party and the Landespartei, he (Mourer) could take Roos's place and control the joint organization. In a 1938 police report, the Communist Autonomists are described as being dependent upon the Landespartei (and the "clerical" autonomists) for success at the polls and as cooperating "intimately" with both the *E.L.Z.* and Bickler's mass youth movement, the Jungmannschaft. Indeed, it was the *E.L.Z.* that announced fusion of the Landespartei, the Communist Autonomists, and the Jungmannschaft on July 29, 1939, just five months after Roos was seized by the French police.[47]

Although a clever maneuverer, Mourer never managed to become a good spy for the Germans. "He didn't make a good impression," said his Abwehr contact, Erich Knabbe, "appearing to be too superficial." (In his denials of being an espionage agent for the Germans, Mourer later admitted that his go-between to Ernst, Albert Bongartz, talked a lot and asked many questions, a "mania" Mourer ascribed to the fact that Bongartz had

once been a teacher!) Professional German intelligence
officers were instructed not to recruit Alsatian autonomists as agents—with several exceptions, as we shall
see. Protecting the autonomists from French reprisals
was not the only reason for this ban; as politicians, neither
Mourer nor Roos nor Bongartz, for that matter, had
much military information to pass on to their German
employers.[48] Indeed, one gets the impression that Ernst
and the other Germans regarded the autonomists as a
group of ineffectual, Byzantine intriguers. Ernst later
testified that they could never have been organized without his help, boasting that he "was the active and
coordinating force of the Alsace-Lorraine battle for the
Heimat against France."[49]

Hermann (Armand) Christian Bickler, the youngest
of the Alsatian autonomist leaders analyzed in this study,
was the only true Nazi among them. He boasted, in fact,
that he was part of the "real *Nazi-group;* that put me in
the front line." Born on December 28, 1905, in Hottwiller
(Moselle) of a German father and Alsatian mother,
Bickler was too young to fight in the First World War
and opted for French nationality in 1919.[50] As a law
student at the University of Strasbourg, he joined the
Heimatbund in 1926 under the aegis of Emile Pinck and
quickly became one of the leaders of the two major
Protestant and German-oriented student organizations,
the Argentina and the Wilhelmtina.[51] Bickler became a
member of the Landespartei in 1929 and, after setting
himself up to practice law with Pierre Bieber in Strasbourg, began to contribute articles to the *E.L.Z.,* the
party newspaper. Starting in 1931, he edited the paper's
supplement, which he called the *Jungmannschaft.* Aided
by Friedrich Spieser and a corps of comrades from the
University of Strasbourg, Bickler transformed the *Jung-*

mannschaft in 1933 into a full-fledged periodical, with a program stressing defense of the national characteristics *(Volkstum)*, particularism, and antiassimilationism. Based on these same goals, Bickler established a youth group, also called the Jungmannschaft. Soon becoming a para-Hitlerian organization, it acquired a slogan-salute ("A free people—in their own country [*Freie Volk—Im eigenen Land*]") and adopted a brown uniform with a black armband inscribed with the Wolfsangel (a nocturnal sorcerer in the form of a wolf); it had marching songs ("To Alsace Thou Must Be True [*Treu dem Elsass sollst du Bleiben*]") and followed the leadership principle *(Führerprinzip)*, with the twenty-nine-year-old Bickler as leader.[52] A 1931 article by Bickler in its journal asked what the use was of learning French.

> French is as foreign to us as Italian or Spanish. Some say, French should be required because it is the language of the State. But we repeat that we do not want to belong to any other than an Alsace-Lorraine state. We don't need to learn any other language than German.[53]

At the same time, a pamphlet (apparently drawn up for the Jungmannschaft by a German agent whom Ernst paid), was placed on the desks of University of Strasbourg law students returning for the spring term: "Put aside that which is corruptly foreign [*Welsch*]. Speak German. . . . Protect your sacred language."[54]

Bickler's view of Alsatian history, spelled out in *L'Histoire d'Alsace-Lorraine,* published in 1935, was that of a German nationalist: compared with the horrors of the French "conquest" of the seventeenth century and the inequities of the current French "occupation," German rule between 1871 and 1918 had been light indeed. Alsace was cheated out of a plebiscite in 1918, Bickler reasoned, and greeted the French enthusiastically only out of relief that the war had ended. "But all attempts

to destroy our national characteristics are bound to fail,"
Bickler wrote. "Our language is spoken by one hundred
million men . . . a free people in its [sic] own land!"[55]
(Bickler denied being the author of this tract when
questioned at Nancy in 1940, but the editor, Frédéric-
Charles Eyer, admitted that Bickler had corrected the
page proofs.)[56]

The Jungmannschaft should not be confused with
the Bauernbund, a contemporaneous Haut-Rhin peasant
organization whose leader, Joseph Bilger, used methods
similar to Bickler's. Bilger worried the police not because
of his politics as much as because of his escapades in the
local taverns. He began his movement in 1935 with a
proclamation against autonomism, but by 1938, the
Bauernbund was parading about in green shirts, giving
Nazi salutes, using stormtrooper tactics against oppo-
nents, and advocating a corporate state. (Bilger was in
contact with Henri Dorgères, the demagogic peasant
leader and a proponent of the "Fourth Republic," in "interior" France during the late 1930s.) A scandal involv-
ing Bilger in a brawl with a prostitute ("fille de mauvaise
vie") in a Strasbourg tavern in 1935 is typical of the
reports on this character in the city's police files.[57]

Unlike the Bauernbund, the Jungmannschaft was an
avowedly separatist organization from its very inception.
Transforming itself into the Elsass-Lothringische Partei
in 1934, with its own newspaper, the Frei Volk, it had
130 sections and some two thousand members concentrated in Bas-Rhin (Saverne, Hagenau, Wissembourg,
and Alsace bossue along the Palatinate frontier). This
new party began to outflank the older, comparatively
staid Landespartei; it was filled with antibourgeois as
well as anti-French propaganda, charging that soon "it
will be too late for the Francophile Alsatian bourgeoisie;
we shall take their places." The Jungmannschaft was
quickly classified by the French police as the most

dangerous pro-German organization in Alsace; it was not autonomist but separatist and had its maximum impact on students, petty functionaries, peasants, and veterans of the German army of the First World War.[58] The Jungmannschaft was one of the first two organizations to be banned by the French government (on April 21, 1939) as war approached. The ban followed a Strasbourg meeting of the group held at the restaurant Maeder on September 19, 1938. At this meeting Bickler proclaimed that although Hitler had officially renounced reannexation of Alsace-Lorraine, the province still had the right to self-determination and charged that the region formed a "German minority" within France.[59] This sentiment echoed the manifestoes published by Bickler since 1936 in which he called for administrative autonomy, an end to the "exploitation" of Alsace and its people by "foreigners" (the French), and "restitution" of the wealth "stolen" from the province. These inflammatory demands were always accompanied by calls for the primacy of the German language in Alsace and resistance to French assimilation.[60] In confiscating documents from the Jungmannschaft's party headquarters on October 3, 1938, the French police found evidence connecting Bickler with Konrad Henlein, the Sudeten German leader, and with Fransez Debauvais, the Breton autonomist chief, and his publication, the *Breiz Atao.*[61]

Bickler dealt directly with Ernst and other Germans and did not have to use Bongartz as an intermediary as the other Alsatian autonomists often did—a source of real discomfort to them. Ernst's father had been the founder of the Wilhelmtina, one of Bickler's student fraternities at the University of Strasbourg; both were devout Protestants.[62] In 1937, Ernst and Dr. Karl Poechel, rapporteur (*Westreferent*) for Alsace-Lorraine affairs at the Verein für das Deutschtum im Ausland, combined forces to help Bickler outmaneuver Roos, Schall, and Hauss for control of the Landespartei. By the end of 1937, Bickler—whom Poechel called the "man of the future"—was triumphant; Roos had been relegated to a nominal role in the Landespartei, which by now had shrunk to the confines of the city of Strasbourg.[63] The next step was a united front of autonomists, a coalition Bickler clearly expected to head. His letter to Rossé in October 1938 pleaded for a unified formation which would include the Jungmannschaft, the "avantgarde of the autonomist movement." Rossé's reply, circumspect as always, was that he would "see what we can do with this matter" at a future meeting which, of course, was never arranged.[64]

Bickler performed exceedingly well for the Germans. He was in contact not only with Poechel and Ernst but also with the Toepfer brothers, Ernest and Alfred, important links to autonomist Friedrich Spieser.[65] Bickler attended all of the autonomists' meetings with Ernst, including the one that misfired in Switzerland in October 1938. But unlike the others, he also gave the Germans valuable military information as an espionage agent (*Sicherheitsdienst*): his reports, apparently, were channeled through Bongartz.[66] What position would Bickler's rival, Jean-Pierre Mourer, hold in the projected united front of autonomists? The latter coveted the top post as much as did the former, and the decision between them was up to their German supporters. For the time being, however, the question of who would be chosen was put in abeyance. On September 4, 1939, Bickler was taken from the French army unit in which he was serving and sent to jail in Nancy as "one of the most active and dangerous" German agents in Alsace-Lorraine.[67] (The army's fortress units had been alerted as far back as 1936 to the menace of Bickler's Jungmannschaft in their very midst.) Imprisoned at Nancy, Bickler would be not quite as arrogant in his separatist role; there is even one indication that he considered turning state's evidence. In a letter to the Juge d'instruction, dated April 1940, he asked for an interview alone, "outside the ordinary framework of an interrogation." (This thought had not prevented Bickler from excoriating Julien Marco as a *mouton* ["stool pigeon"] at Nancy: passing him in February 1940 during a recreation hour, Bickler had snarled, "We must all receive the same treatment as Alsatians. When they have squeezed you like a lemon, they will throw you aside.")[68] But this momentary weakness would be overlooked by the conquering Germans. During the occupation of Alsace, they would impartially and equally reward Bickler and his rival, Mourer, for their prewar services.

Next to Bickler, Freidrich (Frédéric) Spieser was the youngest of the Alsatian autonomists and, like him, was judged in absentia by the French courts after 1945. But unlike any of the others, Spieser was the only autonomist trained in Germany specifically for a role in interwar Alsace; his job was cultural subversion, aimed at returning the area to Germany. Born on October 1, 1902, at Waldhambach (Bas-Rhin), Spieser was the son of Alsatian parents. His father, a Protestant pastor, was described in an official report as a "specialist in cultural and linguistic questions" and characterized by his son as a descendant of "anti-French [*Franzlingen*] peasants."[69] Young Spieser apparently did some desultory study at the University of Strasbourg after the armistice, but left in 1926 for the Universities of Tübingen, Göttingen, and Marburg. He earned a doctorate in letters and philology at Marburg in 1930 for a thesis entitled "The Life of the Popular Song in a Lorraine Village." Spieser dedicated the work to Abbé Louis Pinck, author of a famous collection of German Lorraine folk songs and the brother of autonomist Emile Pinck, Ricklin's associate on the *Zukunft*. On August 24, 1931, Spieser was married in Strasbourg to the Gräfin und Burggräfin Agnes von und zu Donah-Schlobitten, an exceedingly plain-looking member of an exceedingly rich and powerful East Prussian noble family.

Spieser apparently was noticed by Ernst very early in Spieser's career: he writes about "confiding" in Ernst while still living in Alsace, as early as 1926. There is also evidence that Ernst actually paid for Spieser's education in the German universities and supported him before Spieser's marriage made him a wealthy man.[70] The essential point, however, is that Spieser, who had prolonged his university studies in Germany with the single aim of serving Germanism abroad, was ready in 1931 to go back to Alsace to start negotiations with Bickler; these were to culminate in the founding of the Jungmannschaft in 1933 and also to revive the ailing Bund Erwin von Steinbach. This latter organization had been created at the crest of the autonomist tide in 1926 by the pastors Auguste Hirtzel and Maurer and by Professor Eugène Würtz. On arriving in Alsace in 1931, Spieser took over control of the Bund and headed it until it was dissolved (along with the Jungmannschaft) by the French government on April 21, 1939.[71]

But the real reason for Spieser's return to his homeland was Ernst's persuasion that he should undertake a cultural frontal assault on French "assimilationism."[72] On his wanderings through the Bas-Rhin countryside in 1926 with a hiking and singing society he had founded, Spieser had come upon a mountain in the lower Vosges near Saverne called the Hünenburg (Hunabourg). (The actual locality was next to the village of Dossenheim-zur-Zinsel.) It offered a fine view of the Vosges and the valleys leading into French Lorraine. Spieser was de-

termined to "build a real bastion of Germanism there."
Unfortunately, from Spieser's point of view, the land
was owned by a French sympathizer (*Welschling*). But
by a great stroke of luck, financing was at hand. Alfred
Toepfer, the Hamburg and New York shipping and grain
magnate, who was already in contact with Bickler, had
written Ernst early in 1932 of the urgent need to con-
struct a youth hostel for those "who profess their attach-
ment to the hereditary Germanness of Alsace and Lorraine."[73] Spieser—just the man to fulfill the task of
protecting *Deutschtum* in Alsace—was available and so
were the funds.

Putting the two together was a relatively easy
matter, given Ernst's intricate financial connections with
the Alsatian autonomists. On September 7, 1932, Spieser
wrote to Ernst from Kehl, the German city opposite
Strasbourg, that "it is now possible to acquire the land
for a higher price than expected because of other bids:
60,000 francs." (The letter was signed "Otto.")[74] In
a letter to Toepfer, dated September 17, 1932, Ernst
noted, "I should emphasize . . . that I would like to
interpose this person [the notary Eugen Wildi of Zo-
fingen] so that neither my name nor Spieser's appears in
Swiss banks. . . . [Our] adversaries have got wind somehow" of the venture.[75] The rounded amount of 21,000
Swiss francs (the equivalent of 100,000 [1932] French
francs) was duly deposited in Wildi's name in the
Schweizerische Volksbank by the firm Ernest W. C.
Toepfer of New York; Alfred Toepfer, the Maecenas in
the affair, wished "our friend"—Spieser—well.[76] Spieser
was summoned by Ernst to Basel where he was given
60,000 French francs to begin negotiations for the purchase of the site. In addition, he received 60,000RM for
the project from the Verein für das Deutschum im
Ausland (V.D.A.).[77]

Two and one-half years later, Spieser was complaining of lack of funds: rumors published in the Alsatian press, the closing of an access road by the French Forestry Administration, and the forced purchase of extra land for a spring, had together created a dire need for an additional 7,000RM. "This isn't much," Spieser wrote Ernst on April 5, 1935, considering the splendor of the "silent witness to German culture" which had been built on the mountain and named for it, the Hünenburg. The funds Ernst sent in answer to this plea for the lump sum of 7,000RM and an additional 3,000RM per trimester were, apparently, insufficient: the total cost of the castle with its land was 1.32 million French francs.[78] However uncertain about money, Spieser had definite ideas concerning the infiltration (*noyautage*) of Alsatian society (or, as he put it in a vulgar Alemmanic expression, how to "operate evilly for several more years [*ein paar Jahre so weiter gewurstelt wird*]") until the work began to bear fruit. Of this Spieser wrote, "I'm optimistic."[79] Spieser's later and unbearably long memoirs give no indication of this particular mission; they do, however, indicate amply what an idiotic dreamer (*Schwärmer*) or joker (*fumiste*) he really was.[80]

In carrying out his subversive cultural assault on assimilation, Spieser attacked on several different fronts. First, for the youth, who had been neglected during the construction activities—something Spieser regarded as "just as well for political reasons"[81]—he spelled out ten commandments. The "Alsace-Lorraine resistance" must "honor [the] beautiful mother tongue [*Muttersprache*, not *Mundart*] which has always been German." The movement must be "proud . . . and not let [itself] be blinded by those who slavishly and ridiculously imitate the French [*Nachwelschen*] and who are only half-educated"; it must "warn our people against the evil leaders who collaborate with the enemies of the *Heimat*."[82] On another front, Spieser aimed at the formation of a "political and cultural elite." This was the task of a "small circle of friends whose political chief is Hermann Bickler and of which I am the cultural director." "Young doctors, clergy of both confessions, teachers, and others" would constitute this elite. Spieser hoped to involve two other groups: the peasants—"especially the women"— and the "layer of the half-educated," who believed that to "play at being French [*welschen*]" was the height of culture. In exposing these two groups to their own native songs, dances, and dialect, Spieser expected the difference between Alsatian mores and customs and those of the "intruding French [*hergelaufene Welschen*]" to become obvious.[83]

Spieser wanted none of these visitors to know of the ultimate, subversive aim of the Hünenburg, nor should German guests and even the German architect working on the castle.[84] Secrecy was imperative, for

> even if our hearts tell us that we can perhaps once again light bonfires of joy in the Vosges to the sound of all the churchbells of the Third Reich, no one knows how much longer the bitter and corrosive reality of assimilation will continue to destroy our national characteristics [*Volkstum.*][85]

Spieser was anxious not to have the Hünenburg attract special attention. Its heavy construction costs, he felt, could be camouflaged by his wife's considerable personal fortune. It was important to

> shroud the work, give to the enterprise a superficially inoffensive and pleasing aspect. I want very much to appear as the free man who is crazy about hiking. For that reason, I want one day to invite a group . . . from the opposite side. . . . I have always observed how astonished the French are by our songs . . . and dances.[86]

This desire to appear innocuous and nonpolitical explains

why Spieser contacted Marc Sangnier, the French apostle
of the Youth Hostel movement, and why he invited tourists in general and youth groups from Germany, including the Hitlerjugend, to stay at the Hünenburg.[87]
While the French police were under no illusions
concerning the work for *Deutschtum* that went on at
the Hünenburg, the Germans admired Spieser as the
one autonomist of whom they could be absolutely sure.
A 1937 document describes him as "from all points of
view reliable," of "purely pan-German mentality [*rein
Grossdeutsch eingestellt sein*]," and "one of the most
worthy forces for Germanism in Alsace."[88] (Regrets were
voiced in this document over the inability of the German
authorities to release printing paper stock to the monthly
Strassburger Monatshefte, which Spieser had begun to
edit with Ernst's money in 1937.) Spieser, on the
other hand, gave his own opinions concerning Alsace
to his German friends. The growing disturbances
in France were "favorable," Spieser argued, to the
autonomists and the Germans; he felt that the majority of the haute bourgeoisie were now autonomist
and that the Jungmannschaft was currently receiving
support from industrialists. Spieser characterized Rossé
as "pure German in his heart," noting that as a sly
tactician, Rossé sometimes had to criticize Nazi church
policy. Spieser argued that Alsace was not, as some
charged, "faithless and treasonous" but "German-feeling"
in the majority of its population. At this point, Spieser
yearned for a meeting with Hitler or one of his deputies
to "give them the true story" concerning Alsace-Lorraine.[89]

The closest Spieser got to this goal was two years
later, in September 1939, when as a refugee from French
justice, he stayed at the Schlobitten castle, Schloss Wundlacken, near Königsberg in East Prussia. He was not a
Nazi party member: although a later account has Spieser

buying his first swastika in 1920 and being "very clearly for" the führer in 1937, Spieser did not enter the organization until well after the German conquest of Alsace, on January 1, 1942.[90] Despite this handicap, Spieser felt free to write an excruciatingly long letter to the führer describing in detail the great "need" of Alsace, reeling under the "assimilation and extermination policies" of the French. Although loyal to France during the crisis of 1938, Spieser argued that neither he nor Alsace was "French any longer." A plebiscite should be held to determine whether Alsace wanted autonomy or a protectorate status under German rule; many Alsatians, he felt, would work loyally for Hitler. Germany must no longer abandon Alsace as it had in 1681 and 1815: "Mein Führer! I beg your protection for my presently hard-pressed and wounded ancient German homeland [*Heimat*]. Your will can make us free. Long live the Third Reich!"[91]

The recipients of this plea, however, were unimpressed. Otto Meissner, chief of the Reich chancellory, describing Spieser as "head of the German movement in Alsace," passed the letter on to Martin Bormann. The only reaction thereafter was an explanatory note placed in the file by Emile Otto Paul von Rintelen. Stating that after the "extraordinarily categorical clearing up" of Hitler's speech on October 6, 1939 (in which Hitler denied any interest in territorial cessions by the western powers), von Rintelen explained that only a "war of life and death" would permit the subject to be developed further.[92] How close the "fastest possible reattachment [of Alsace] to Germany"[93] was, of course, no one except the führer could know. Within nine months, the wildest dreams of Spieser, Ernst, and their associates would be fully realized.

To complete this picture of Alsatian autonomist leaders between 1919 and 1939, let us briefly review Robert Ernst's activities. Of the numerous Alsatian-oriented organizations which Ernst either directed or to which he belonged, the most important were the Bund Deutscher im Westen, founded in 1933, and the venerable Verein für das Deutschtum im Ausland. Throughout his memoirs and court testimony, Ernst insisted that the aim of all these groups was cultural autonomy for Alsace within the political framework of France. It is possible that some members of one of these organizations, the Hilfsbund der Elsass-Lothringer im Reich, hoped for German reconquest, but officially Alsace's reversion to French control was "considered definitive." Certainly the German government itself would never have permitted "particularism" to develop into irredentism, openly threatening the security of a contiguous state. In his postwar memoirs, Ernst even described his work with the autonomists as "honorable."[94]

Such innocuous goals were hardly the whole story, of course, as the evidence of German political and cultural infiltration of French Alsace indicates. Several items in Ernst's dossier also contradict his assertions. The Elsass-Lothringisches Wissenschaftliches Institut an der Universität Frankfurt-am-Main, an allegedly cultural organization, was inaugurated by Ernst himself in a speech in 1921 in which he described it as an "arsenal within which will be forged the arms necessary for this combat [of *Deutschtum* between the Rhine, Moselle, and the Vosges]."[95] A series of letters written between July 5, 1939, and May 2, 1940, reveal too that handsome subsidies were given to the Bund Deutscher im Westen by the German Ministries of the Interior, Foreign Affairs (Section VI), and Propaganda and by the Bund deutscher Gemeindetag.[96]

The loan to Spieser for the Hünenburg by the Verein

für das Deutschtum im Ausland (V.D.A.) has already been mentioned; this group also figures in an audit made of Ernst's Berlin organizations in November 1937 as having received 1 million RM between 1933 and 1937 from the Ministries of Finance, Foreign Affairs, and the Interior. Adding this amount to the dues paid by its "millions" of members makes the V.D.A. by far the most powerful irredentist force in both Weimar and Nazi Germany. It held annual drives resulting in receipts of several million marks.[97] And Ernst's connections with the Reverend Emile Scherer were, according to the Alsatian autonomists themselves, much more intimate than the merely "cultural" ones Ernst claimed to have had.[98]

In any case, Ernst was known as Germany's outstanding expert on Alsatian questions. His party membership and his opposition to the anti-Nazi president of the V.D.A., Hans Steinacher, endeared him to authorities in the Third Reich. It was, therefore, not surprising that with the coming of war Ernst should be named technical councillor for Alsatian affairs in the Foreign Office. He had "no precise mission" other than to contact those who would be involved in a future occupation of the province; according to his testimony, he did not get in touch with any Alsatians or with any Germans residing in Alsace.[99]

Ernst did learn that two colleagues from the SS were already preparing for the police administration of Alsace a list of those considered reliable (*Wahrleute*) in the area. Nevertheless, Ernst was shocked by a speech of Josef Bürckel, chief of the Civil Administration of the First Army in the Lorraine sector; in it, Bürckel referred to Alsace as "German territory." Hitler had renounced territorial acquisitions in the west in his speech following the conquest of Poland on October 6, 1939. Ernst felt that Alsace-Lorraine should preserve its integrity and have a special statute resembling the 1911 constitution.[100]

Within six months, however, even this German concept of limited autonomy would be swept away and Alsace incorporated into the district (*Gau*) of Baden under an *Altkämpfer* ("old fighter") associate of the führer, Robert Wagner (né Backfisch). And Ernst himself, as Wagner's assistant, would state, "The Alsatian autonomist movement was justified as long as there was no German Reich, but today with Hitler, this Reich is a reality [and] the question of an autonomous Alsace within the framework of the Reich no longer exists."[101]

4

War, Occupation, and Liberation: 1939 - 1945

Most of the autonomist leaders—Bickler, Mourer, Hueber, Rossé, Stürmel, Bieber, Brauner, Hauss, Keppi, Lang, Lefftz, Meyer, Schall, and Schlegel—spent the *drôle de guerre* (1939–40) in the Nancy prison; Spieser had fled the country in August 1939 to stay with his wife's East Prussian relatives. Karl Roos, who had been arrested on February 3, 1939, many months before the others, was condemned to death on October 24, 1939, by the military tribunal on charges of high treason; he was executed at Champigneulles, near Nancy, on February 7, 1940. Would other autonomists face the same fate as this future martyr of the "Alsace-Lorraine resistance"? Some of them surely must have feared for their lives. Writing later to Ernst, Mourer averred, "In those hours when we lay in prison and began to hope, you were the person to whom all our hopes were directed."[1] But such morbid thoughts were really without basis, at least for the time being.

Although the autonomists were kept under strict confinement (Stürmel, in a "reinforced cell"), their interrogation (*instruction*) dragged on at the tortoise-like pace of a government whose offensive against Germany was not scheduled to take place before the spring of 1941. Leads were not followed through, especially in the questioning of Stürmel: much information on him had been given by Abbé Brauner. Especially in the case of Bickler, who was a lawyer, investigators permitted themselves to be outwitted by clever tactics. *Aux écoutes,* a sensational Paris weekly, asked its readers in April 1940 whether a "serious inquiry" was ever to be conducted into the affairs of those who enjoyed "powerful protectors."[2] Nevertheless, while the autonomists were in jail, confessions were made and information revealed—in particular by Julien Marco, possibly by Bickler, but also by Jean-Pierre Mourer himself. Mourer later claimed that by the end of the winter of 1939–40, he was definitely suspect in the eyes of Bickler and Schall, whose lawyers had recounted Mourer's disclosures linking them with Ernst, Roos, and Bongartz.[3]

The autonomists—*Nancéens,* or *Nanziger* as they would soon be called—were hastily evacuated to Lyons on June 14, 1940, as the German panzers began to encircle Nancy. From there, the prisoners were transferred to Valence on June 16, then to Avignon on June 17, to Mende (Lozère) on July 1, and finally on July 2 to Privas, capital of Ardèche, some six hundred kilometers from Paris. After Hitler demanded the autonomists' release from French custody, they were sent on July 14 to the nearest German army unit, stationed at Châlons-sur-Saône. Their captivity had lasted 281 days, and they were about to enter the last, sorry act of interwar Alsatian autonomism.

Their mentor, Robert Ernst, was waiting for them at the mountain-top resort of Les Trois Epis, above Colmar. Ernst was head of the para-Nazi party group in Alsace, the Elsässische Hilfsdienst; on June 30, 1940, he had been named councillor for Alsatian affairs by the German secretary of state for interior affairs, acting on the order of Hitler himself. Ernst was to work with Robert Wagner, a participant in Hitler's Munich putsch in 1923, a former captain in the Reichswehr, and Gauleiter of Baden since February 1925; Wagner had just been named Gauleiter of the combined region of Baden-Alsace. According to his own testimony, Ernst was determined to "prevent the complete inundation of Alsace by the people from Baden," and to reward the "pioneers of Germanism" with high governmental posts "in the interest of the Alsatian population." In reality, however, by agreeing to serve the Third Reich in this new position, Ernst had aligned himself with Hitler, who was as firmly opposed to Alsatian autonomism as the French had ever been. Furthermore, Ernst intended to force the autonomist leaders to renounce publicly their century-long struggle for Alsatian particularism. In the bargain, Ernst would appear to be their leader and could thus counterbalance the power of his fractious superior, Wagner.[4]

So the *Nancéens* were not allowed to go free when they crossed the new frontier—the 1871 border—into Alsace. On Ernst's orders, they were kept in confinement by German army units at the Trois Epis for forty-eight hours until, after some wrangling, a pro-Nazi resolution addressed to Hitler was drawn up and issued on July 18, 1940. Along with Ernst, Bickler, Mourer, Rossé, and Stürmel, Antoni, Bieber, Brauner, Hauss, Keppi, Lang, Meyer, Nussbaum, Oster, Schall, and Schlegel signed the document. It read:

> Today, the pioneers of our Alsatian and German Lorraine peoples, . . . liberated from French prisons, have arrived on Alsatian soil.
>
> They committed only one crime: that of remaining faithful to their *Volkstum* [national characteristics]. . . . Peace and justice, understanding between the French and German peoples, was the aim they sought despite the burden of their souls until France, in a criminal fashion [last phrase crossed out and replaced by "with an unheard-of blindness"] began a war against the

German people and therefore rejected definitively this
effort full of renunciation.

United with these men, tens of thousands . . .
assembled in the Alsatian Hilfsdienst . . . and, with
them, hundreds of thousands [of others] ask that [you]
proceed today to the integration of their *Heimat* within
the Great German Reich, remembering Dr. Karl Roos,
executed by French bullets.[5]

The declaration was flown to Berlin the same day,
where Ernst submitted it to Dr. Heinrich Lammers,
general secretary of the Reich Chancellery, for inclusion
in Hitler's speech the following day. But the führer had
not changed his ideas concerning Alsace since the Freudenstadt (Baden) conference of June 20, 1940. Hitler
wanted to keep the matter of Alsace's reannexation in
suspension for the time being, meanwhile installing a
complete German civil administration in the province.
Although in his speech Hitler mentioned the Posen and
Westpreussen situations as comparable to the Alsatian
one, it is clear that he was engaging in the opportunism
and improvisation typical of his whole approach to re-
arranging the post-1939 map of Europe.[6] He made no
mention at all either of the autonomists' declaration or
of the future of Alsace. Ernst had to return to Colmar
empty-handed, with only the news that the area was to
be treated as a de facto annexation of Germany's, but
without any proclamation or statement to that effect;
all of the elaborate celebrations planned in Bas-Rhin and
Haut-Rhin to greet the news of reannexation had to be
cancelled. All Ernst got by way of explanation was
Wagner's assertion that a secret convention in the
Rethondes armistice agreement between France and
Germany provided for retrocession of Alsace to the
Reich, but that because of Hitler's eagerness to enlist
French aid in the struggle against Britain, no public
revelations of the measure were to be made.[7]

Why did men who had devoted their careers and risked their lives for autonomism suddenly and completely renounce their convictions? First, certainly, because of the rapidity and completeness of the German conquest of France. On every side, they were told that for all practical purposes the war had ended. What could they, representing the interests of tiny Alsace, do before the German monolith, especially when they had been told that France had given the province to Germany?[8] Nevertheless, there had been serious differences of opinion in the tense negotiations at the Trois Epis, and, as he later confessed, Ernst had to use "threats" and "pressure on the consciences" of the "quarantined" *Nancéens* to overcome their objections.[9] Rossé, Stürmel, Keppi, Oster, and Brauner demanded that the phrase "criminal fashion"— used in the draft resolution to describe the Daladier government's declaration of war on Germany—be stricken, that France publicly consent to German annexation, and that the Alsatian people should be asked to approve the step. Rossé, Stürmel, and the others also insisted that religious and local liberties be guaranteed by Germany. Rossé later claimed that it was because of these "reservations" that the Trois Epis declaration was not made public by Berlin.[10] Bickler, Mourer, Bieber, Schall, Hauss, Lang, Meyer, Nussbaum, and Schlegel offered no opposition to the document; Bickler and Bieber were so pro-German that they even maintained that the word "renunciation," in the second paragraph of the manifesto, meant giving up an "intimate desire" to be reannexed to Germany. Mourer later confessed that he supported the separatist side, fearing repercussions from his revelations at Nancy, but objected to the claim that the group had the power to draw up such a manifesto. In his mind, he averred, was the memory of the 1918 renunciation of a plebiscite by the Landtag deputies, a decision bitterly criticized by many Alsatians between the wars and one which had become a political red herring.[11]

Discussion of the document grew so bitter that at one point the faction led by Rossé left the meeting room by crawling out the windows—the doors were barred by German soldiers. The autonomists soon returned, however, when informed by Ernst that German treatment of the Alsatian population depended upon their "attitude" toward the manifesto.[12] Convinced, too, that a refusal to sign would bring the Nazi antireligious legislation to Alsace, Rossé finally dropped all his objections but one. He insisted on substituting the phrase "unheard-of blindness" for "criminal fashion" to describe French action in September 1939.[13] The troublesome question of the "legality" of the German reannexation of Alsace had made its first appearance, but the era of autonomism under French rule was at an end; and the autonomist leaders themselves had renounced their ideals under German pressure.

The history of the German occupation of Alsace, the "secret annexation,"[14] during the Second World War can readily be divided into two parts: the first extends from the fall of France in June 1940 to August 25, 1942, when the conscription of Alsatian males into the German armed forces was declared; the second runs from the conscription edict to the final liberation of Alsace in 1945.

Conditions for an acceptance of German rule in Alsace were far from unfavorable during the summer of 1940. First, most of the population understood and spoke German: in 1940 14 percent spoke only dialect; 70 percent spoke dialect and German; 16 percent spoke dialect and French.[15] Second, there was genuine relief at the end of the fighting and the return of Alsatian soliders from German prisoner-of-war camps. There was even hope that the region would somehow be autonomous under the new masters. One of the prime sources of public opinion during the occupation, the famous war journal of Professor X., records such hopes. On June 14, 1940, and as late as January 3, 1941, Professor X. of Colmar, an A.P.N.A. sympathizer and fierce anti-Nazi, wrote, "If Germany understood our situation and if she let us decide our destiny, she would have enormous sympathy in the land."[16] There were indications at first that the Germans were determined to avoid the mistakes made between 1871 and 1918. For example, a Sicherheitsdienst report, another valuable source of public opinion, dated June 27, 1940, revealed a nice understanding of the Alsatian problem: the inhabitants, "thrown back and forth" between the powers, were not "characterless and without honor"; of necessity, they had adopted a "wait and see" attitude. The report urged that great care be taken in the choice of Reich officials in Alsace: no Prussians or North Germans, but only those with sympathy for borderland problems.[17] Compared with this wise advice, the reports of the Deutsches Ausland-Institut were foolish and dangerous. They insisted that French influences be completely rooted out with force and that Alsace be immediately incorporated into the Reich because the "dynamism of the Führer and his movement . . . has worked faster and more thoroughly here than 'anyone' ever expected."[18]

As summer turned to fall and the refugees evacuated from Strasbourg and the Ried (the area north of the capital) were repatriated from Périgueux,[19] the Germans began to tighten their grip on the "recovered" Reichsland. The Hitlerjugend and other Nazi youth groups were brought into Alsace on September 8, 1940; expulsion of the French and of the Jews proceeded, as did confiscation of their property; the Nuremberg laws were introduced. Eradication of French signs and of the

French language was decreed, accompanied by the Germanization of Alsatian names and a ban against wearing the *béret basque,* an allegedly "French" cap. The local currency was converted into reichsmarks at a disastrous loss to the province; the compulsory work law (*Reichsarbeitsdienst*) took effect on May 8, 1941.[20] By this time, with Britain still resisting and the war extended to the Soviet Union, the tone of the secret police reports darkened. Hostile feelings toward the Germans made their first appearance; some sympathy for the Jews persisted, although there was "in general in the province a latent anti-Semitism."[21] Catholics kept their children away from Nazi youth activities; de Gaulle and La France Libre (Free France) grew in popularity; in Haut-Rhin, anti-Nazi incidents indicated "planned activity by a Francophile group."[22] These reports were echoed in Professor X.'s journal, emphasizing a point made at the time in a Deutsches Ausland-Institut document: Nazi sympathizers accounted for no more than 20 percent of Alsace's population; the rest were opportunists (*Stellenjäger*).[23]

But the worst was yet to come. On August 25, 1942, after a conference at Vinniza between Hitler, Keitel, and Wagner, the conscription of Alsatian males between the ages of sixteen and thirty-four was decreed—upon whose initiative, it is still not clear.[24] Wagner boasted that Alsace had "turned positively toward the Reich" in a kind of "plebiscite," that he had the "total confidence" of the province, and that he was its "spokesman." In his opinion, Alsace had legally been annexed by Germany by virtue of a secret accord with France at Rethondes which Hitler never published because of his "great respect for Pétain."[25] Wagner told Ernst of this secret treaty which "suppressed Versailles" and convinced him too that conscription was legal.[26] With Hitler's decree, therefore, conscription was possible and, indeed, necessary because

voluntary enrollments had proved extremely disappoint-
ing from Germany's point of view. "In a totalitarian
state," Wagner later testified, "one can govern only
totally."[27]

Before August 1942 neither Wagner nor his associate, Ernst, had been known for their severity in the administration of Alsace. Indeed, Wagner had intervened
unsuccessfully to save a young France Libre resistance
fighter from execution,[28] and he had avoided carrying out
Hitler's orders to expel and transplant one-third of the
Alsatian population left after the banishment of the Jews
and the French. Wagner later testified that by this
measure Hitler "wished to solve the Alsatian problem
definitively and radically. He did not tell me the reasons
for this order."[29] Ernst, although plagued by his denunciation of a Strasbourg hairdresser for speaking
French, had generally helped his pro-French relatives
and their friends in the anti-German ruling class (*Oberschicht*), on which the Deutsches Ausland-Institut reports dwelt. Ernst testified later that his denunciation
was meant only as a warning to Madame Wittersheim,
and not as an order for deportation; he claimed that the
whole affair was "painful" to him and an exception to
his general attitude toward the Alsatian population.[30]

Nevertheless, the Germans, and Ernst specifically,
had promised the Alsatians that their sons would never
be mobilized for service in *Wehrmacht* (armed forces)
units.[31] Ernst objected to conscription for "psychologi-
cal" reasons, "as an Alsatian; afterward, the German
citizen took over."[32] To set an example of dutifulness for
the Alsatian public and for high party officials, who were
also being called upon to make sacrifices for the Fatherland at this time, Ernst left his post as Wagner's assistant and as mayor of Strasbourg shortly after the conscription decree to take up service as a non-commissioned
officer in the east. From there he wrote articles appealing

to the loyalty and courage of the young Alsatian conscripts.

Mass resistance was not long in coming, and it
sprang from much more than mere "enemy radio propaganda," as Wagner later claimed. On the night of
February 13, 1943, fourteen young Alsatians tried to
escape conscription by crossing the Swiss border near
the village of Ballersdorf in the Sundgau; in a melee, one
of the German customs guards was killed. Without the
requisite formalities, all fourteen were taken immediately
to the Struthof concentration camp where, despite the
pleas of their lawyers and of Ernst himself, they were
executed three days later, on February 17.[33]

Meanwhile on February 14 and 15, riots broke out in
the Haut-Rhin villages of Kaysersberg and Orbey over
the conscription of Alsatians into the German army; some
five or six hundred persons were involved. Wagner, who
justified the Ballersdorf executions on the grounds that
"hundreds more" would desert if the captives went free,
condemned one person from the rioting crowds and one
of the rebellious conscripts to death in order to make an
"example" of what resistance to the conscription edict
would cost. These sentences were carried out on February 25, 1943, after Wagner had addressed a large,
captive audience in Colmar on the "Bolshevik menace"
and the "extirpation of treason without mercy."[34] The
myth, the "tragic comedy," of Alsace as faithful to the
Reich was henceforth destroyed: of the 130,000 conscripts drawn from both Alsace and Lorraine during the
war, 35,790 were killed, including some 10,500 lost without record on the eastern front.[35]

What was to be the fate of the autonomist leaders
during the German occupation? First, Ernst had to find
something to do for the *Nanziger* once they had been

liberated from their Trois Epis prison; they were prestigious figures, after all, and they had just publicly recanted their mission in life by rallying to the German annexation. In his testimony given after the war, Ernst claimed that he had urged Wagner to install a "special system relying largely on Alsatians" to govern the recovered province, but that the Gauleiter, seduced by the apparent enthusiasm of the masses for reannexation, refused to adopt his project, citing the example of the refractory years before 1918, when Alsace had a semi-autonomous status. Instead, Wagner agreed to a tabula rasa of all Alsatians' past political attitudes, except for the French "of the interior" who were to be expelled. (A German report in February 1941 calculated that 169,221 fewer people were living in Alsace then than on March 8, 1936. Of that number, 95,327 were "undesirables"—Jews, French, French sympathizers, and others —who had either been expelled or had not returned; 35,180 Alsatians were employed in the *Altreich* [pre-1939 Germany]; 7,484 foreigners had not returned. Only 31,320 people were available and "suitable" for repatriation from Vichy France.)[36]

Despite the Gauleiter's rejection of his plan for the *Nanziger,* Ernst had a reserve card to play. Upon arriving in Colmar on June 20, 1940, he had created—and headed —the Elsässicher Hilfsdienst, originally conceived of both as a mutual-aid society and as a "grouping of Alsatians in the place of the [Nazi] Party." The Hilfsdienst also processed the release of Alsatian soldiers from German prisoner-of-war camps; the condition of liberation was the signing of a statement that the individual concerned was an "Alsatian of German blood [*Volksdeutscher*]." The Hilfsdienst provided semi-official positions for the leaders, and soon all of the autonomists were given important posts: Rossé was named rapporteur for culture and propaganda; Mourer became chief of workers' af-

fairs; Bickler was in charge of personnel; and Stürmel
was made chargé d'affaires for Haut-Rhin agriculture
and food supply. Spieser, who had just returned with
the victorious Wehrmacht, was placed in charge of *Kul-
turpolitik*. As such, Spieser was at least partially responsible for a notorious poster put up all over Alsace; entitled
"Alsace Protests against France [*Anklage des Elsass
gegen Frankreich*]," it was a violent diatribe against the
political, racial, cultural, financial, and economic "crimes"
of France.[37] Although the Hilfsdienst rapidly became a
cesspool of agents provocateurs and was dissolved officially early in 1941, more anti-French propaganda
followed.

Ernst sent the most prominent members of the
Nanziger out on the hustings to give pro-German
speeches under the rubric of the "great turning point of
our time in Alsace [*Die grosse Wende unserer Zeit im
Elsass*]." Joseph Rossé gave four major talks for the
Nazis during the summer of 1940 at Colmar, Guebwiller,
and Mulhouse, while Marcel Stürmel spoke at Altkirch,
Thann, and elsewhere. In these speeches and in the
Elsässer Kurier, both men thundered against the "rob-
bery" that France had perpetrated on Alsace for twenty
years, extolled Roos as a *Vorkämpfer* ("early battler") for
German Alsace, and counselled that the "Hans-im-
Schnockeloch" era for the province was over for good.
The "Hans-im-Schnockeloch" phrase comes from a popu-
lar rhyme that refers to the alleged Alsatian dissatisfac-
tion with whatever the region has at any given moment:

> Hans in the mosquito-hole has everything he wants.
> And what he has, he does not want, and what he wants,
>   he does not have,
> Hans in the mosquito-hole has everything he wants.

> D'r Hans im Schnockeloch het alles was'r will.
> Un was'r het, des will'r nit, un was'r will, des het'r nit,
> D'r Hans im Schnockeloch het alles was'r will.[38]

Mourer and Bickler were even more intensely anti-French, as Mourer tried to outdo Bickler to compensate for his own disclosures at Nancy the previous winter.[39] These two and the other *Nanziger* were rewarded late in 1940 with a special, week-long visit to victorious Berlin, where they were greeted by Otto Meissner, chief of the Präsidialkanzlei des Führers, in "good Alsatian-German [*guet alsässer-ditsch*]." (Meissner was born in Alsace of German parents before 1918.) They then visited the various Reich ministries, including that of Himmler, who took them to the Sachsenhausen concentration camp where, "in conditions of absolute cleanliness where severe discipline reigns, they were able to see how false were the reports circulated from abroad on these camps."[40]

By the end of 1940, the status of the *Nanziger* had become almost symbolic. In 1941, they were assembled in Strasbourg for a "day of the Alsace-Lorrainers in the Reich," during which a portrait of autonomist Georges Ricklin was unveiled and a street named after him. Beginning in December 1940, Wagner and Ernst held an annual dinner for them; this banquet became more Lucullan the lower rations for the rest of the population sank. In a period of relative penury, December 1943, the *Nanziger* enjoyed pâté de foie gras and the very best Alsatian, Bordeaux, Burgundy, and Champagne wines. The Gauleiter gave majolica bowls to the autonomists' wives; the men received books with such titles as *Jewish Ritual Death [Der jüdische Ritualmord]* (Schramm) and *The New Faith [Der neue Glaube]* (Gericke).[41] The *Nanziger* were brought out in force to attend the solemn ceremonies surrounding the return of Roos's body from Nancy to Strasbourg on June 19, 1941. They became "honorary citizens" of the newly reopened German University of Strasbourg on November 23, 1941, the anniversary of the French troops' 1918 arrival in the city. And the autonomist leaders were all given German nationality on August 24, 1942—the day before conscription into the German armed forces was decreed for Alsatian males.[42] This meant, of course, that they were now subject to conscription.

Ernst did not succeed in securing for the *Nanziger* status as deputies to the Reichstag in Berlin, although he went so far as to draw up a list with Spieser and Bickler representing the Jungmannschaft; Schall, the Landespartei; Mourer, the Communist Autonomists, and Rossé, the U.P.R.[43] But Ernst did achieve his goal of placing almost all of them in the new German administration in Alsace. Some obtained very high posts indeed: this was an era, as Wagner later ruefully confessed, in which everyone wanted an official position.[44] Bickler was named Kreisleiter of Strasbourg; Mourer, of Mulhouse; Lang, of Saverne; Nussbaum, of Molsheim; and Hauss, of Hagenau. Rossé was made chief of the Indemnification Bureau for "pioneers of *Deutschtum*" in Alsace. Stürmel, who was less easy to place than the others, was finally given the post of fourth adjunct mayor and municipal councillor of Mulhouse. Abbé Joseph Brauner retained his post as director of Strasbourg's Municipal Archives; Dr. Joseph Lefftz became head of Strasbourg's Municipal Library; and Dr. Joseph Oster kept his position as director of Strasbourg's Municipal Hospital.

All the autonomists were viewed, as least initially, in a favorable light by the German authorities. Mourer was described by Wagner as "without a doubt, a good German, a good National Socialist, a good orator, and full of zeal," and Bickler was lauded as "not only a good German, but a good National Socialist . . . [and] also a very good Kreisleiter."[45] Even Rossé and Stürmel, with their clerical ties and religious concerns, were "German in their attitudes and true to their homeland [*deutschbewusster und heimattreuer*]" and had "served the cause so well that one must have understanding for and patience with their difficult position." By 1943, this appraisal of the two had been reversed: Rossé and Stürmel were condemned for "ultramontanism," in the tradition of Abbé Haegy, and labeled as "sworn enemies" of National Socialism.[46]

As before the war, Rossé was the most circumspect of all the autonomists in his dealings with the Germans. It is true that he made certain concessions to the new order. After his duties as district orator (*Gauredner*) ceased in the fall of 1940, he became head of the Indemnification Bureau; in that position he apportioned more money to his old autonomist comrades than to the comparatively recent interlopers like Spieser. Rossé also became municipal councillor of Colmar in August 1941. His article in the *Kolmarer Kurier* of October 19, 1940, entitled "The 'Traitors' of Nancy," detailed his secret relations with Roos and how he had helped Roos before his execution in February 1940; it also denounced the French inspectors, Becker and Léonard, and thanked the German armed forces for his liberation. (After the war, Rossé claimed that the German editor of the newspaper invented the article from "objective" notes which Rossé had furnished.)[47] It was Rossé who expressed gratitude (in Alsatian dialect) for the entire group to Otto Meissner when the *Nanziger* visited Berlin during late November and early December of 1940. (Rossé claimed later that he undertook the Berlin trip to protest expulsions from Alsace, but realized only after his interviews with dignitaries in the German capital that "the traditions . . . and the mores of our fathers" were to be eradicated, and that the Nazis would also undertake the "violation of the Alsatian soul and the destruction of our ethnic personality.")[48]

Despite these revelations, Rossé petitioned Ernst for entry into the Nazi party and was admitted on January 27, 1941.[49] He wrote Wagner on July 6, 1941, about his readiness to relinquish his mandate as a French deputy: "After all that France has done to me, another attitude would be incomprehensible. . . . I led the battle for German *Volkstum* for twenty-two years and endured many trials and eighteen and one-half months of prison." (Although Rossé could not deny this letter later on, he claimed that his life was in danger at the time and that he never sent the necessary note of resignation to the *questeur* ["general administrator"] of the Chamber of Deputies.)[50] And, finally, Rossé indemnified himself for "material losses [suffered] in the struggle for *Volkstum* in Alsace" to the amount of 18,000RM, to which an appreciative German review board added 8,500RM as compensation for his dismissal as a primary school teacher by the French and 4,500RM for his incarceration at Nancy.[51]

But Rossé also occupied himself, much more than the others, with the relatively uncontaminated world of business: as Paul Mass, the German mayor of Mulhouse, exclaimed at Rossé's postwar trial, he was "first and foremost a businessman!"[52] He became director of the Central Bureau of Foreign Insurance Companies on September 4, 1940, and a director of the Société générale alsacienne de banque the same year. His primary business interest, however, was as head of the Alsatia publishing empire, replacing Xavier Mappus, who had been dismissed by the Germans. On assuming his functions in August 1940, Rossé announced that "in regard to the new situation, [Alsatia] feels itself to be, and functions as, a German publishing house, but it relinquishes none of its fundamental Christian bases."[53]

At the cost of portraying Alsatia as the "defender of Germanism in Alsace" and of printing pro-German and anti-French broadsides, Rossé was able to prevent his house from being taken over by the Hünenburg publishers or by the Propaganda Office of the Baden-Alsace district. He was able to keep almost all of his personnel out of either German military or civilian service, to protect the company's stock held by those "in the interior," to acquire the *Elsässer* of Bas-Rhin in order to save it from confiscation by the Nazis, and to delay the sale of Alsatia's Colmar printing plant until December 31, 1944, by which time the Germans were fighting for their lives in the city. In the bargain, he was also able to prevent the destruction of French books owned by Alsatia and to print anti-Nazi and religious books and catechisms which were distributed underground throughout the Reich—a total of 2,107,606 copies according to Rossé later testimony.[54]

Wagner was completely ignorant of Rossé's maneuvering (*double jeu*): he described him as one who "collaborated with us loyally, without conditions . . . he was a good German. I had no confidence in Rossé as a Nazi but . . . did as a German."[55] Amazingly enough, Rossé accomplished all of these tasks with great profit to Alsatia and, incidentally, to himself. The company's receipts for 1943 were 211,178RM, and Rossé's salary for the entire occupation period amounted to 96,033RM, to which was added 300,000 French francs for expenses and 121,446.40 francs in Alsatia dividends. In addition, Rossé received 2,000RM annually from his insurance and banking activities and a monthly stipend from the German government to cover his salary as a French deputy after Wagner issued the edict forcing all former parliamentarians to relinquish their French political status.[56] All of this was in keeping with Rossé's ability to maneuver and to emerge the victor from a difficult situation: nothing illicit had been done; in comparison with the rest of autonomists, he was relatively unblemished by

Nazi contacts and, in the process, wealthy as well. But despite the success of what Robert Schumann, a postwar leader of the Mouvement Républicaine Populaire and architect of Franco-German reconciliation, later called Rossé's "opportunism,"[57] he was fated to share the post-liberation purge (*épuration*), just as he had had to endure prison at Nancy, with the most ardent pro-Nazi autonomists of the day.

The complexity of Rossé's activity in response to the second, savage phase of German occupation in Alsace illustrates the dilemma in which he and the other autonomist leaders found themselves. They were now leaders without a cause. Rossé did not protest the conscription edict, leading Wagner to assert later that Rossé's

> attitude . . . influenced me indirectly to propose to Hitler German military service in Alsace . . . [and] contributed to persuade me that the majority of Alsace was German. I never had the impression that Rossé played a double game and that he retained relations with France. . . .

Rossé's answer was that he could not protest or challenge a decision by Hitler, that

> idol for whom he [Wagner] had an insane devotion. . . . It is understandable that Wagner, because of my unfortunate incarceration at Nancy in 1939–1940 . . . assumed that I was a good German. In my numerous interviews in favor of my compatriots with him . . . I could not present myself as a *maquisard* or a Gaullist. . . .[58]

And there is evidence to show that Rossé's activity on behalf of condemned persons (those to be deported into the Reich) and the families of those who escaped conscription was at least moderately successful.[59]

While not connected to the local resistance networks, Rossé did regularly pass on information regarding Alsace to Pétain through Bernard Fay, the Vichyite head of the

Bibliothèque Nationale in Paris. Rossé emphasized that, from the Alsatian point of view, the German situation was "desperate over the long run" and pointed out measures which the French could undertake to "utilize and accentuate the irresistible current of public opinion against Germany." Some of this information was forwarded to the resistance network Mithridate and to the Free French in Algiers.[60] These activities led Rossé to assert after the war, while on trial for his life, that he "undertook the most extensive action against the Third Reich by an Alsatian residing in our province," that he "sabotaged" German efforts in Alsace in "vast proportions."[61] Such a statement, although ignored by his judges, has a curious relevance when placed within the context of Rossé's efforts on behalf of autonomism.

Was Rossé reasserting the principles of autonomism, or rather neo-autonomism? It is important to remember that he distrusted the Germans as "elephants in a china shop" and as perverters of the Alsatian *Volkstum*, which, he maintained, included religious elements and functioned within the "internal politics" of France.[62] The Germans, of course, repaid him in kind: a 1944 propaganda report sent to the Gestapo chief of Alsace condemned Rossé for indulging in "Jesuitical language," and he was generally regarded as suspect by the Nazi party.[63] At first, Rossé was convinced that France "had abandoned Alsace to Germany" by a secret clause in the armistice agreement (and in the compromise peace which soon followed) and that Alsace should form a buffer state (*état-tampon*) with the Rhineland, Belgium, and Luxembourg.[64] He attempted to contact United States Embassy officials in Paris concerning this project during the fall of 1940, but was unable to reach them until June 1942 when, through the Papal Nuncio to France, Monsignor Valerio Valeri, Rossé was introduced to the U.S. Embassy at Vichy, which reported on his plans to Washington. During a conference between Roosevelt and Anthony Eden in March 1943, the president brought up the subject of Wallonia, a new region to include Walloon Belgium, Luxembourg, Alsace-Lorraine, and the Pas-de-Calais area of France. In his memoirs Eden wrote, "I recorded at this point that 'I poured water, I hope politely, and the President did not revert to the subject.' "[65]

During the period between July 1940 and November 1942, Rossé made many trips to Vichy, attempting to interest the French authorities in "real autonomy" which he was "sure" would be granted by the Germans. His reception at the temporary French capital was cool, if not frigid. A hostile official report on his démarches conceded that some support for Rossé's ideas could be found—not because of anti-French feeling in Alsace, but because of "lassitude, [people] thinking that the new regime would bring them some peace and a less uncertain future."[66] Nevertheless, Rossé was immediately declared "undesirable" in the Unoccupied Zone by France's defense minister, Léon Huntziger, a fellow Alsatian.[67]

What backing there actually was in 1941 and 1942 for Rossé's brand of autonomism is difficult to establish. A royalist document of the time states that Alsatians did not want Germany as an overlord any longer, but that "we are disgusted with France." Even Professor X.'s journal, which vehemently opposed Rossé's autonomism as a cheap trick to buy popularity and redeem his "treason," complains of the "lack of understanding" in—and a-bandonment by—"the interior." In one of its more impassioned passages, the journal declaims:

> Our Alsatian history will judge you [Rossé] later on very severely! It was you who sowed the whirlwind and you see now what you reap. By your primitive spirit and your unbridled ambition . . . you have troubled people's minds for years, divided the people and the

clergy. . . . You have betrayed what is most sacred for a
province: the union and love of the great motherland![68]

Whatever the audience for neo-autonomism might
have been, by the end of 1943 Rossé was playing both
the German and the French ends off against the middle.
On the one hand, he told his associates that a German
defeat and Alsace's reattachment to France were inevitable: it was no longer a question of "autonomism or
regionalism; he even accepted [the certainty] that the
special regime of the clergy in Alsace [i.e., the Concor-
dat] be abolished."[69] On the other hand, Rossé was
engaged in protracted negotiations with the German
resistance over a program for returning Alsace to France
and, during the transition period providing for the immediate suppression of the Nazi party, the arrest of all
war criminals and denunciators, the expulsion of all
German immigrants, the freedom to speak French, and
the return of all deportees, Wehrmacht conscripts, and
forced laborers. These terms were approved by the
German resistance and by Klaus von Stauffenberg himself in an interview with Rossé in Berlin sometime during
March or April of 1944.[70] After the abortive plot of
July 20, 1944, Robert Wagner, representing high Nazi
party interests, informed Rossé through intermediaries
that, as Gauleiter, he would have no objection to Alsace
as a neutral state. Rossé, however, asserted that he would
"never commit such treason against the Alsatian people
who want only one thing: to become French again."
Neo-autonomism was dead; in Colmar on December 2,
1944, Rossé narrowly escaped capture by the Gestapo
and deportation across the Rhine to Baden.[71]

Compared with Rossé, the political and business
activities of the other autonomists were far less complex.
Early in the occupation Stürmel began writing obsequi-

ous articles in the *Elsässer Kurier* ("Why Alsace Thanks
Germany and Her Führer [*Warum dank das Elsass
Deutschland und seinem Führer*]") and boasting that
his connections with the Elsass-Lothringisches Institut
an der Universität Frankfurt-am-Main had served the
cause of *Deutschtum* for fifteen years.[72] He also immediately applied to Ernst for party membership and to the
Waffen SS recruiting bureau in Strasbourg for SS membership. Stürmel was accepted into the party but not
into the SS, despite his insistence that he was an "Alsatian
of German origin."[73] Both applications were accompanied by a pro-German vita (*Lebenslauf*) in which he
described the armistice of 1918 as "one of the most
painful trials of my life"; Stürmel also asserted that he
had created the "revolution conceived here in Alsace
. . . long before the national revolution in Germany"
and that "this land wishes . . . eternally to be in the
great German Reich."[74]

Stürmel's application for monetary indemnification
as a "pioneer of Germanism" in Alsace was more successful. His old friend and political associate, Joseph Rossé,
as head of the Indemnification Bureau, saw to it that
Stürmel was eventually rewarded handsomely for the
losses suffered because of the sanctions taken against
him as a signer of the Heimatbund manifesto, his incarceration at Colmar, his trial for claims of war damages
in 1937 and 1938, and his imprisonment at Nancy. In
fact, Stürmel was awarded 9500 French francs more than
he asked for; part of the damages he claimed pertained
to the 1926 loss of his (deceased) wife's job in the post
office. This compensation, and his pro-German activities,
explain the description of Stürmel in Professor X.'s journal as the "most odious" of the autonomists.[75]

Stürmel was described by his colleagues, however,
as generally "correct" in his dealings with his subordinates at Mulhouse, where he was an assistant mayor and

a municipal councillor.[76] Indeed, it seems that he retained his post only with the support of Kreisleiter Mourer against German attempts to eject him from office. (Despite his pro-Nazi attitudes, Stürmel—a "clerical"—was suspect in their eyes.)[77] After Stürmel's early and rather clumsy attempts to influence and counsel Wagner had failed, he, like Rossé, did not object to the conscription edict. Gauleiter Wagner later maintained that Stürmel's silence "contributed to the conviction that I possessed the confidence of the Alsatian people."[78] As with Rossé, however, Stürmel's later interventions in favor of deserters, resisters, and deportees were sometimes successful. Although obliged to use obsequious language ("My great aim is and remains to bring back . . . this frontier people to the Great German Reich"), Stürmel wrung from an unwilling Wagner the concession that deserving cases be exempted from the mass deportation of some four thousand people conducted as a reprisal for the Ballersdorf border-crossing incident.[79] And through contracts in Vichy, including Nuncio Valerio Valeri, Stürmel aided in influencing Hitler in March 1943 to commute the death sentence of the Strasbourg artist, writer, and resistance activist, Robert Heitz, to life imprisonment.[80]

Stürmel's contacts with Vichy, in comparison with Rossé's, were quite restricted; the most notable incident occurred in July 1941. During a visit to Pau to arrange for the repatriation of a home for the Alsatian aged, Wagner threatened Stürmel, promising dire consequences if he, like others in his situation, did not immediately resign his seat as a French deputy. After much delay, Stürmel sent a draft letter of resignation to Wagner, but the *questeur* of the Chamber of Deputies never received it.[81] The question of who emerged as the victor in this tug-of-war between Stürmel and the Gauleiter is open: Stürmel received his back pay as a deputy

from September 1939 until September 1941; thereafter
the German government continued to send him a monthly sum as compensation.[82] Like Rossé, Stürmel found it
profitable to be an ex-deputy in German Alsace; again,
this explains the venom of condemnation of him in
Professor X.'s journal.

The Germans had no problem in placing Bickler in
their new administration of Alsace. Although Wagner
had originally preferred Paul Schall as Kreisleiter of
Strasbourg, he came to believe that Schall was more
valuable as chief editor of the *Strassburger Neueste
Nachrichten,* formerly the pro-French *Dernières Nouvelles de Strasbourg.* The paper's first edition under
German rule, published July 8, 1940, contained an article
(by Fritz Kaiser) asserting that the French persecution
of those loyal to the *Heimat* was still "too little" known
in the Reich.[83]

Bickler had entered the Nazi party on January 1,
1940, while still a prisoner at Nancy, probably through
the good offices of Ernst and his Sicherheitsdienst friends.
Named Kreisleiter of Strasbourg on September 10, 1940,
Bickler was sent to train under Kreisleiter Willy Fritsch
of Freiburg-im-Breisgau and assumed his duties in
Strasbourg on January 1, 1941. Seven months later, on
July 5, he was also named Kreisleiter of Kehl as part of
Wagner's program to weld Alsace and Baden into a
single political and economic unit.[84] But between times,
Bickler had also entered the SS as a *Standartenführer*
(colonel) on September 6, 1940, a move that was eventually to save his life.[85] In addition, he kept up his links
with the Sicherheitsdienst (security service) in Strasbourg, pressing—among other things—for the extradition
of French police commissioners Becker and Léonard, his
prewar enemies, and for punishment of the chief of the

Nancy prison guards and his wife who had been responsible for "odious" treatment of the autonomists during the winter of 1939–40.[86] "No one knows better than you how strongly I try to collaborate . . . with you and your services," Bickler wrote the Sicherheitsdienst, who responded with testimonials of praise for his contributions to their cause.[87] Bickler was also awarded the large sum of 18,200RM by Rossé's office as an "indemnity for losses suffered during the struggle for Germanism in Alsace."[88]

As Kreisleiter of Strasbourg, Bickler employed a half-conciliatory, half-threatening attitude toward the population under his control. He sought, for example, the release of all those, including the ringleaders, involved in pro-French demonstrations in Hochfelden on July 14, 1941.[89] On the other hand, he denounced three families whose sons had fled obligatory work service in January 1942. Bickler also issued a veritable cascade of orders to his deputies (*Kreisleitung*) that a "radical cleansing" of French street signs, billboards, and names be carried out. His circulars extolled the ultra-short German haircut (*Kulturschnitt*) and the "beautification of our streets and squares by obliterating the last traces of the foreign rule of the French." One sign which aroused Bickler's ire read "Essolube und Magic-Hôtel!" Delinquent officials were threatened with dismissal.[90]

During the later period of the occupation, Bickler was known, above all, as a recruiter for the German military. "All young men," he announced to a meeting of SA members of his district in March 1942, "should long ago have been made soldiers! Only the life at the front . . . can have [a] quick and deep effect [on them]. . . . They constitute racially and humanly an exceptional natural resource" for the army.[91] At the end of the year, he put himself and his brother-in-law, Rudolf Lang, Kreisleiter of Saverne, at the disposition of the German armed forces for front line duty. Bickler held himself up as a dutiful example in a speech to young conscripts: although he had been deprived of his cherished family during his incarceration at Nancy, he was leaving them again to fight for the Fatherland.[92]

This heroic posture, however, was merely a sham, as high officials in Strasbourg discovered to their great displeasure in January 1943.[93] Bickler—and with him, Lang—had obtained sinecures for themselves; Bickler would not be in the battle lines of the eastern front, but in Section VI of the Sicherheitsdienst in Paris. After joining the Reichssicherheitsdienst Hauptamt (RSHA) in Berlin for training, Bickler rose rapidly through the ranks to colonel, a promotion whose swiftness was a direct consequence of his affiliation with the German intelligence service before 1939. Section VI of the Sicherheitsdienst (located on the boulevard Flandrin in Paris), which he headed from early 1943 on, specialized in political intelligence in France, Spain, Portugal, Switzerland, Britain, and the United States. It controlled the intelligence service of the French fascist organizations, Doriot's Parti Populaire Français and Bucard's Francistes, and of Joseph Darnand's notorious Milice. Through his preparations for intelligence networks to function during the coming Allied invasion and his training of French and German agents who were to remain in France "after the war," Bickler quickly assumed great influence in collaborationist circles, in the naming and treatment of French functionaries in the Laval government, and in the orientation of German policy toward Vichy.[94] While Bickler himself wielded no repressive powers, he was, of course, in constant contact with Section IV of the Sicherheitsdienst—the Gestapo.

Bickler was arrested by Wehrmacht units in Paris on July 20, 1944, the day of the abortive plot on Hitler's life, but was quickly released after the plot miscarried. Bickler left Paris for Strasbourg on August 11, where he directed the local Sicherheitsdienst and its Milice followers.[95] In September of that year, he was named chief of the southwest command post (Leitstelle Sudwest) of the RSHA (sometimes called "Sonderstab West"): using the cover name of Walther in Baden-Baden, Hornberg, and Hellingenberg, Bickler concentrated on penetrating the French administration in the newly liberated areas of Alsace. When the end of the war came there, he was arranging for the flight into Spain of Alain Laubreaux and Charles Lesca, two writers for the arch-collaborationist French newspaper *Je suis partout*.[96]

At the beginning of the occupation, Spieser again became editor of the *Strassburger Monatshefte*, which merged with Ernst's *Elsass-Lothringen Heimatstimmen* in August 1940. He also founded a publishing house, the Hünenburg Verlag, on Wagner's initiative in the spring of 1941 to educate the Alsatians in the "philosophical concepts of National Socialism" and to "provide a spiritual bastion against the west."[97] Although his lifelong goal, German cultural subversion of Alsace, had been reached, he continued to build at the Hünenburg, adding a guest house early in 1941. When Himmler visited the Hünenburg on September 6, 1940, he made Spieser a *Sturmbannführer* in the SS.[98] But Spieser was not a member of the Nazi party, a fact which greatly irritated him and made him resent those Alsatians who had already been accepted into the party's ranks. Writing to Paul Schall on October 28, 1941, Spieser complained that in the past he was "more important to the French than certain people who strut around with the Party insignia, while a Spieser has to wait a long time to be found worthy. But enough of this trifling dirt [*kleinen Dreck*]. . . ." Schall replied consolingly, agreeing that "what you say about our earlier efforts, namely that these

should be more strongly emphasized, is also my opinion.
We succeeded [in a task] which many Party members in
pre-1939 Germany [the *Altreich*], far away, did not have
the opportunity of handling, a fact which should be
emphasized."[99]

Spieser was eventually received into the party on
January 1, 1942; his "attitude toward the Jewish question" was described as "very good." Although considered
"one of the Alsatians most hated [by the French] because
of his militant conduct," Spieser's attempts to obtain a
settlement of 89,506RM from the Indemnification Bureau
for his fantastically detailed accounts of "corruptly foreign [*Welschen*] vexations and dirty tricks" fell on deaf
ears.[100] The bureau, under Rossé's leadership, revised
Spieser's estimates of damages downwards by 10,000RM
and then rejected his petition altogether on the grounds
that he had already received more than enough German
funds to build a sound investment. Rossé asserted that,
in contrast to other "fighters for the homeland"—for example, Roos's widow, Bickler, and Keppi—Spieser had
a secure material base and ample monetary resources.
This was a pointed and specific reference to Spieser's
having spent the winter of 1939–40 in comfort at Schloss
Wundlacken in Germany, not in prison at Nancy. Spieser's petition was certainly not helped by the fact that
at the time the Hünenburg Verlag was attempting to
take over Alsatia, Rossé's own publishing empire.[101]

Over the next few years, Spieser wrote repeatedly
to the head of the administration and police in the civil
administration for redress of his grievances. He invented
the whole idea of bringing Roos's body back from Nancy
to the Hünenburg, a temporary resting place while a
mausoleum was built at the Place Kléber (Karl-Roos
Platz) in Strasbourg.[102] Spieser sent Christmas packages
with the Hünenburg calendar to his SS comrades, "with
comradely SS greetings (*mit SS-Kameradschaftlichen*

Grüssen)."[103] And he drew up fantastic memos to "dislocate" France by annexing Burgundy, all of Lorraine, Flanders, and Normandy. The soil and climate in these areas, similar to that in Germany, was "excellent," Spieser reasoned, and volunteer colonists of "healthy blood" could be settled there as compensation for their efforts to aid the Fatherland. These projects were necessary, Spieser wrote, to defend the Reich against the United States and to create a Germanized Europe; for as long as France existed, it would, in the name of "Western culture, liberty, and civilization, remain the focus of those who think in European terms. . . ."[104] But despite these proofs of party orthodoxy and his indignant pleas that the French should not be allowed to "escape from their guilt" and receive a "gift" by not being forced to pay him, Rossé's tribunal replied that "moral damages" could not be compensated; the most the bureau would grant Spieser was 24,000RM. The sum was immediately sent to the indignant chatelain of the Hünenburg.[105]

By this time—January 4, 1944—there were more serious matters on everyone's mind: German Alsace itself was in jeopardy. Also by this date, because of his disillusionment with the Indemnification Bureau, the party, and the increasingly harsh occupation, Spieser had become dangerously hypercritical (a *frondeur*) in Wagner's view. Spieser's savagely satirical article on the Gauleiter's administration in the April 1942 issue of the *Strassburger Monatshefte* had caused a sensation in Alsace.[106] Spieser had written letters to Strasbourg inveighing against the expulsions and deportations to France: "We must cure the sick Alsatian soul."[107] He had even entered into negotiations with some of Rossé's neo-autonomists.[108] At the end, Spieser was definitely suspect in the eyes of the Gauleiter.

Jean-Pierre Mourer's original acceptance of Wagner's offer to become Kreisleiter of Mulhouse, the second largest city in Alsace, was motivated by the fear that Bickler had alerted the Gestapo to his confessions made at Nancy during the winter of 1939–40. His old political comrades, including Hueber, also advised him to go to Mulhouse, although he later testified that "all my political past" was contrary to accepting the post. Mourer immediately applied for and obtained membership in the party as SA *Oberstürmbannführer* (lieutenant-colonel), boasting that his pre–1939 manifestoes were the "first testimony of the Alsatian people against French authority that they wished to be German."[109]

During the first part of the occupation, Mourer compiled a record in Mulhouse quite like Bickler's in Strasbourg. The weight of evidence in his postwar trial dossier, however, emphasizes Mourer's increasingly severe policy as the war went on: rabble-rousing pro-Nazi speeches at official rallies; public approval of conscription; the Ballersdorf executions; and mass deportations of the families of draft evaders and French sympathizers, especially around Saint-Louis.[110] On the other hand, Mourer later maintained that the population of Mulhouse "understood" his "double game," and defense witnesses attested to his numerous interventions to save individuals from the Gestapo and to his serious differences—in private—with Wagner over official policy.[111] One thing, however, is certain: Mourer, the individual, underwent a personality change as Kreisleiter. Gone were the pious days of prison in Nancy when he composed hymns to the Virgin. Now, his fondness for orgies and carousing in Mulhouse taverns became part of the regional folklore, as did his liaison with a Viennese singer at the Muncipal Opera of Mulhouse; he finally married Gertrud Jahoda five months after their son, Hans Dieter, was born on March 19, 1944.[112] (The first Madame Mourer, Jeanne

Neufeld, had left him in 1938 because of his many infidelities and had emigrated to the United States.)

Mourer's last act as Kreisleiter was, as might be expected, sheer farce. Instead of heroically organizing a mass flight of his subordinates and their families from the Caserne Barbanègre in Mulhouse when the troops of de Lattre de Tassigny's First French Army came pouring into the city on November 20, 1944, Mourer merely got drunk and slipped out into the sortie of some twelve hundred people escaping to the German lines behind the Doller.[113] Meanwhile the French troops proceeded to go in other directions for different objectives. At this point, testimony differs as to Mourer's fate: by one account he was praised by Wagner for his heroic action at Mulhouse and was subsequently set up at a new Kreisleitung headquarters at Mülheim in Baden. Another account has Wagner trying to bring him before a military court and have him shot for inaction.[114] In the twilight period between the end of fighting in Alsace and the surrender of the Reich, Mourer's followers waited in vain for him, first at Bantzenheim (Haut-Rhin) and then at Mülheim, but Mourer had simply disappeared into thin air.

Of all the administrators, it was Ernst whose policy exhibited the most dramatic change during the occupation. After returning from his temporary duty in the east, in June 1943, Ernst became increasingly severe in his dealings with the municipal employees under his jurisdiction. He enforced the oath of loyalty to the führer and the Reich, in part, he claimed later, because his Strasbourg administration was "suspect" in German eyes for not having been sufficiently "purged" in 1940.[115] As a *Standartenführer* (colonel), he made speeches in favor of recruitment into the SS. He refused to intervene

in favor of an engineer of the Electricité de Strasbourg
who was captured by the Gestapo after having tried to
escape conscription. Through Wagner, Ernst also obtained the deportation of another Electricité de Strasbourg employee who had resigned his post as party cell
leader (*Zellenleiter*) in 1943 because of pro-French sentiments. In at least one case, Ernst intervened personally
to ensure that a young Alsatian was enrolled in the German army.[116] While there is some evidence to indicate
that high-ranking Nazis close to Hitler, especially Bormann, condemned Ernst as a "man of moderation" in
Alsace, at home Ernst was branded as an opportunist
who, in order to retain his position, did not "dare" to
oppose Wagner's draconian edicts.[117]

Ernst's reversal of policy took place against a background of steadily increasing gloom and loss of morale
in Alsace. One of the first in a series of Sicherheitsdienst
reports on Alsace stated that only 10 percent of the
population was fully persuaded of German victory after
the Normandy invasion of June 6, 1944: the "wait-it-
outers" were swinging over to the opposition. By August,
the *Stimmung* ("morale") was "extraordinarily bad,"
with hopes of victory at "zero." The next report had
morale at an "absolute zero," with even party members
and leaders showing signs of hopelessness. The last two
reports in the series record a "worsening" of morale; they
concluded that *Volksturm* ("people's storm troop") units
would not be battle-ready for months and that 90 percent
of Alsatians between the ages of sixteen and sixty-five
were "knocking themselves out" to escape serving in
them.[118] The final Gestapo teletype on the Alsatian situation, sent November 20, 1944, reported that "no riots
on the part of the populace" were taking place; there
was fierce fighting still in the Mulhouse sector; and the
first indications of enemy concentrations in the Saverne
area were being reported as the tape was cut off.[119] Three

days later, despite Ernst's last-minute efforts to form *Volksturm* battallions of his city employees, the French Second Armored Division had planted the tricolor on the spire of Strasbourg's cathedral.[120] Ernst and Wagner, narrowly escaping capture by the fast-moving French armored column, fled across the Rhine at Neuf-Brisach. Except for the epilogue of the Colmar pocket, the history of German Alsace was over.

days later, despite Himmler's last minute efforts to form Volkssturm battalions of its able-bodied men, the French Second Armored Division had planted the tricolor on the spire of Strasbourg's cathedral. Ernst and Wagner, narrowly escaping capture by the fast-moving French armored columns, fled across the Rhine at Neu-Breisach. Except for the epilogue of the Colmar pocket, the history of German Alsace was over.

5

Arrest and Trial,
1945 - 1947

In August 1941, Kreisleiter Bickler received an anonymous France Libre tract which read:

> The hour of judgment approaches. Prepare yourself. You will pay the price of your treason. . . . Your account will be settled to the last centime. . . . In allying yourself with the *Boches*, you have dug your grave, for you deserve twelve bullets in your gut. . . . We shall avenge France. Vive la France Libre![1]

A poem was attached to the tract, set amidst a "V" for victory and the cross of Lorraine. Bickler, unconcerned, had sent the missive to the Sicherheitsdienst and promptly forgot about it. But now the hour of "avenging" France had arrived, and the Alsatian autonomist leaders would soon learn what it would mean to them.

The first to be apprehended were two, ironically, who had the least to fear from the returning French and from Allied sympathizers in Alsace, or so it seemed at the time. Joseph Rossé, who had gone into hiding in Colmar in December 1944 to escape deportation by the Gestapo, surrendered to French authorities the day that city was finally liberated—February 7, 1945. The French, supposedly, were hot on his trail, for they—in the person of a hostile Huntziger—had sent his Nancy dossier to Algiers in 1941 for safe-keeping.[2] But, unaccountably, Rossé was not arrested until May 17, 1945, when he was transferred from Colmar to the internment camp at Pithiviers (Loiret). Marcel Stürmel also surrendered voluntarily to French authorities. Accompanied by a friend, ex-Senator Médard Brogly, Stürmel turned himself in at the *sous-préfecture* of Mulhouse on April 16, 1945.[3] He was taken to Colmar and, after several days there, transferred to Drancy, near Paris; at the end of August, Stürmel was moved again to the Tourelles internment camp in the capital itself.

Robert Wagner, who had been broadcasting propaganda messages to liberated Alsace from Baden during the winter of 1944–45, was more difficult to capture. He was ordered by Bormann on March 25, 1945, to stay in his Gau (which had now been reduced to Baden) and organize guerrilla operations from the Schwarzwald; in April he moved to Rippoltsau and then, after a few days of desultory campaigning with nonexistent units, went on to Schonwald, near Triberg, where all his papers relating to the district of Baden-Alsace were burned. His next move was to Bodmann on the Bodensee. There, on April 29, 1945, after dismissing his staff, Wagner attempted to join one of the Schwarzwald guerrilla units his assistant Gauleiter was supposed to have created. En route north, Wagner changed his mind and left the area on July 25, 1945, to join his brother at Lindach; he traveled as Heinrich Graf with a false name and false identity card. Upon arriving, Wagner learned by chance that his wife had committed suicide while being held at the French prison of La Santé in Paris; he then decided to give himself up to the Americans. Wagner was arrested on July 29, 1945, by the 100th C.I.C. unit of the 100th Infantry Detachment at Stuttgart. Before being turned over to the French, he was interrogated by an American intelligence officer, B. B. Giniger, who wrote of his captive, "One can consider the subject as a man of superior intelligence, dangerous for Allied security because of his ferocious fidelity to Nazi ideology."[4]

Although Robert Ernst's odyssey also ended in surrender to the Americans, it was somewhat different from that of his erstwhile superior. Because Wagner had refused to make him mayor of Colmar while the city and its environs remained in German hands (known then as the "Colmar pocket") between November 1944 and February 1945, Ernst did not return to Alsace. Ernst claimed that the Gauleiter had acted out of spite, recognizing too late the correctness of Ernst's more moderate stance when the two had served together in Strasbourg. So Ernst remained in Oberkirch (Baden), directing a shelter and information exchange service for Alsatian refugees and soldiers. The remnants of the Germans' Strasbourg city administration were located at Haslach, also in Baden. Ernst signed the so-called Elsässiche Freiheits-Front (Alsatian Freedom Front) manifesto on December 16, 1944, addressed both to the liberated population and to those still under German occupation, for he was convinced that Hitler's secret weapons would eventually win the war.[5]

Ernst saw Wagner for the last time on April 20, 1945, when the Gauleiter authorized him to join the Wehrmacht. He went south to Radolfzell with Jean-Pierre Mourer (who had unaccountably turned up in the meantime); there Ernst learned that the unit he had intended to join had already signed an armistice agreement with the French. Together, Ernst and Mourer fled to Landeck in the Tyrol; from there they went to Munich on May 5, 1945, where they were given refuge in the house of Karl Bloch, a Jew whom Mourer had extricated from a concentration camp in 1938 with Ernst's help.[6] When regulations were posted announcing punishments for those harboring Nazis using false names, both Ernst and Mourer turned themselves in to the American C.I.C. unit in Munich on August 3, 1945.

Whether they actually concealed their identity to the Americans is a matter of some dispute. Mourer later declared that he was "determined to tell all the truth and to hide nothing concerning my activity before or during the war," but the pretrial judge (*juge d'instruction*) noted in their dossiers that both Mourer and Ernst wished to "disappear in the mass of Nazi personages interned in civilian camps."[7] In any case, the vigilant French inspector Léonard found Ernst in the American internment camp at Altenstadt near Schongau (Bavaria) on March 16, 1946. During his transfer to Strasbourg, Ernst confessed to his French captors that Mourer was also living in the same barracks from which he had just been taken. Ernst made this move because Mourer allegedly had insisted upon "having his situation cleared up by the authorities of his country."[8] Mourer subsequently was located by Inspector Léonard, but "because of certain [unnamed] administrative difficulties," he was not delivered over to the French until July 25, 1946, when he was arrested at Wildbad and transferred to Mulhouse.[9]

A warrant for Hermann Bickler's arrest was issued by the French authorities in Strasbourg on December 8, 1945: along with Schall, Oster, Schlegel, Nussbaum, Lang, and Hauss, he was accused of having secret dealings (*intelligences*) with the enemy. Spieser was also indicted on the same charges that day, but both he and Bickler had vanished. Bickler's whereabouts remain a mystery to this day. Spieser, as he so fulsomely tells us in *Tausend Brücken*, joined the flood of refugees in northern Germany, hoping—like Ernst and Mourer—to escape identification in a mass of humanity.[10] His wife, who initially did not know where Spieser had gone, was located in the castle of the Princess von Salm at Lisch near Darmstadt, but Spieser himself had simply disappeared.

Wagner's was the first case to be examined by the French authorities. For reasons that are not clear, they had agreed, when the former Gauleiter was delivered to them by the Americans, not to execute him before the close of the Nuremberg trials and to return him to United States law-enforcement officers if his trial took more than six months. Wagner proved to be a willing and, at times, a surprisingly naive witness considering he had been the lord of Alsace for more than four years during the war. In early February 1946, when confronted with proof of atrocities at Struthof concentration camp and elsewhere in his former district, Wagner "wept and was overcome with emotion," claiming that he would have undertaken sanctions against the perpetrators of such crimes had he known about them. Neither Hitler nor he "ever desired German supremacy over the entire world," he maintained; the "ideological battle fought by Germany [had] degenerated into madness and horror," he admitted, but "Hitler's relation to atrocities is absolutely mysterious to me." Himmler, a cruel man of "Mongolian characteristics," had had a "pernicious influence," Wagner said, on the führer.[11]

Shortly thereafter, Wagner was placed in the prison hospital for one month. He and several of his associates were found guilty of crimes against humanity on May 3, 1946; in August, when Ernst wanted a deposition from Wagner attesting to his own clemency during the occupation, prison authorities replied that this would be impossible because Wagner was "subject to nervous crises and cries continually."[12] On August 14, 1946, Robert Wagner (né Backfisch), the former Reichsstatthalter and Gauleiter and Hitler's intimate companion during their incarceration at Landsberg prison in 1924 and 1925, was shot at Fort Ney near the Wantzenau in Strasbourg; according to legend, his ashes were scattered in the Rhine. Mourer's trial at Mulhouse was the next to receive maximum attention from the French. The court rejected a defense motion that it be named incompetent because the Tribunal of Nancy, which had examined Mourer's case in 1939 and 1940, had not yet officially turned those records over to the Mulhouse court. Mourer denied having had relations with a foreign power or its agents before June 16, 1940, and denied having received money from any such agents. He did admit, however, that he knew Karl Roos, that the *E.L.Z.* had obtained funds from the Reich, and that it had been his duty as a French deputy to inform his government. "I regret not having done this" was Mourer's statement. As for acts committed after June 16, 1940, Mourer admitted only those facts beyond dispute: having signed the Trois Epis manifesto and having accepted the Kreisleitung of Mulhouse— both, he maintained, on Ernst's suggestion. "But in the exercise of my functions," Mourer testified, "I caused no harm to those over whom I had administrative powers."[13] Eighteen witnesses then testified for the prosecution, eight for the defense. All swore to the validity of the evidence given in their pretrial statements.

To three of the prosecution's questions—did Mourer, in peacetime, damage the external security of the state by entering into relations with agents of a foreign power; was he guilty of having done the same thing on national soil between June 16, 1940, and the liberation; and was he guilty during the war of conspiring with a foreign power—a majority of the jury replied affirmatively. The jury gave no reply to the question of extenuating circumstances.[14] Mourer's sentence, passed on February 28, 1947, was death, national indignity, and confiscation of property. (The ordinance defining "national indignity," issued on August 26, 1946, specified that "unworthy conduct" during the occupation be punished by forbidding the guilty person to hold public office, vote, teach, or bear arms.) After the general prosecutor refused to submit his case to the Supreme Court of Appeals (Cour de cassation), Mourer was shot at 4:40 A.M. on June 10, 1947, at the rifle range of the Ile Napoléon in the commune of Rixheim, along with another condemned man. Both bodies were buried in section VV of the Catholic cemetery in Mulhouse.[15]

Rossé's case was transferred from a military to a civilian court on August 11, 1945, and then moved from Nancy to Colmar; the reason apparently was that the 1940 trial at Nancy had not yielded "positive results" from the French point of view.[16] During the public trial in June 1947 (which, as always in French law, followed a lengthy interrogation [*instruction*]), defense witnesses testified to Rossé's good works during the war and praised him as a "hero of the Resistance."[17] However, Rossé's erstwhile autonomist colleague in the Chamber, Camille Dahlet, testified that autonomism before the war meant "full political and economic," as well as administrative, independence. Accusations by various witnesses, denied by Rossé during the *instruction*, were added to the record. Police Commissioner Monnard described the accused as the "cleverest, most dangerous agent of Germany."[18] On June 10, as the prosecution demanded hard labor for life, a shaken Rossé learned that Mourer had been shot.

The jury found Rossé innocent of the charge of having relations with a foreign power and its agents before the war and guilty of having those relations during the war, but it also found extenuating circumstances in these two guilty counts. This decision was in keeping with the general tenor of judgments handed down in Alsace after the war: compared with France as a whole, more guilty verdicts as a percentage of the Alsatian population were rendered, but because of the exceptional conditions of the region's incorporation into the Reich, fewer death sentences were passed than in the country as a whole. Rossé was sentenced to fifteen years of hard labor, twenty years of *interdiction de séjour*, and the confiscation of his property—real estate, investments, savings accounts, and personal possessions. When Rossé received news of this verdict, he was "wordless and unmoved"; the *Dernières Nouvelles de Strasbourg* editorial commented that the Rossé chapter was now closed and Alsace's return to France was more necessary than ever.[19] Four years later, when Rossé died in prison from cardiac disease, there was no comment in the Alsatian press save *L'Humanité's* description of him as the region's "Pétain." This epithet brought forth an immediate reply from *Le Républicain du Haut-Rhin*, which cited the prewar support Rossé had received from the Communists.[20] Joseph Rossé, with all his faults, was comparatively the most estimable if not the most typical of the Alsatian autonomists; he died a forgotten man.

At first the authorities had trouble locating Stürmel after they placed him in the internment camp of Tourelles in Paris. Inquiries to the camp of Pithiviers (Loiret) brought an indignant reply from the commandant who stated that his camp was not a prison.[21] Finally, Stürmel was rediscovered, sent to Fresnes on December 19, 1945, and from there back to Mulhouse. The police described him at the time as "affable" and as having a "good" moral character, not "addicted to alcoholic beverages" or to *libertinage* or *débauche*, but a "notorious Germanophile and autonomist" nevertheless.[22] The Nancy court had already turned over its powers to the Colmar court by the time Stürmel made his first appearance before the pretrial judge on January 15, 1946. Stürmel represented himself as a U.P.R. deputy anxious for administrative, but not political, autonomy; he denied having separatist leanings. At his public trial in July 1947, Stürmel was found guilty of having had relations with the enemy and having damaged national security both before and during the war. As in Rossé's case, however, the jurors found extenuating circumstances, and Stürmel was sentenced to eight years of hard labor, twenty years of *interdiction de séjour* and national indignity, and fined 330,000 francs.[23] The court rejected Stürmel's appeal motion and, to underline its findings, decreed that he be put on the *fiche* (list of those to be followed) of the Gendarmerie Nationale when he arrived at the central prison of Varaigne at Epinal. In another exceptional move, the court ordered that public notice of Stürmel's sentence be posted in *Le nouveau Rhin français.*[24]

From a very early date, Stürmel began agitating for a reduction of his sentence because of time already served at Nancy in 1939, at Drancy, Tourelles, and Fresnes in 1945, and at Mulhouse in 1946 and 1947. The commissioner of prisons agreed to deduct the Nancy and Mulhouse stays, but not the time spent in "administrative" detention in Paris.[25] On February 13, 1951, a presidential decree reduced all sentences by the time served before conviction, so Stürmel was freed on April 29 of that year. He was forced, however, to live in Dôle; Alsace was still forbidden to him; and he remained under the shadow of national indignity—that is, he could not hold public office, vote, teach, or bear arms. Finally, following a new amnesty law passed by the Chamber of Deputies on August 6, 1953, the Colmar court decided that the "circumstances of the time and place" of the Trois Epis manifesto did not add up to "deliberately favoring the action of the enemy army," although the fact of signing was still "unacceptable." It decreed further that while Stürmel's newspaper articles were "hateful" toward France, they did not aid enemy police or spies, or cause torture, deportation, or death.[26] Stürmel was then declared qualified to fulfill the requirements of the recent amnesty and was allowed to return to Altkirch as a private citizen, where he lived quietly until his death in December 1971—forgotten, like Rossé.

Ernst's case was perhaps the most bizarre of all. His interrogation was the longest and the most fruitful of all those examined here; it went on year after year without a trial ever being held and a verdict reached. This delay was due to the fact that the French authorities believed Ernst to have French nationality; and thus the counts against him included treason, plotting against the external security of the state, and provoking Frenchmen to commit treason. The Appeals Court (Cour d'Appel) of Nancy finally ruled on January 13, 1954, that Ernst did not have French nationality by virtue of his service in the German army, beginning August 21, 1939, and his participation in the Polish and French campaigns of 1939 and 1940.[27] Ernst was immediately granted provisional liberty. But instead of being taken to Stuttgart, where he was to be under the jurisdiction of the War Crimes Service in Baden-Baden, he was sent to Toulouse and then to Nancy on January 20, 1954, for a new trial and another interrogation—this time as a German citizen. External pressure may have been partially responsible for the decision to retry Ernst in France: among the many letters protesting the grant of provisional liberty was one from the political deportees of Schirmeck and Struthof-Natzwiller. They urged the rapid condemnation of Ernst as being responsible (along with Wagner) for the "incorporation and deportation of Alsatians."[28]

A finding of insufficient cause (*non-lieu*) by the Supreme Court of Appeals on February 6, 1954, overturned the Nancy court's refusal to reinstate Ernst's provisional liberty; he was still kept in custody, however, until a new indictment against him was filed on March

9, 1954.[29] After his various appeals to have these new charges dropped had been rejected, Ernst was finally tried and convicted on January 13, 1955. The sentence was eight years of hard labor, the confiscation of property, and twenty years of *interdiction de séjour*.[30] Because his eight years of hard labor had already been more than served in prison, he was taken to the German border and released forthwith. Since that time, Ernst has lived on the Chiemsee, south of Munich; like the others, he is a forgotten man.

Bickler, who had been arraigned in Strasbourg in 1945, was tried in absentia and convicted on September 4, 1947—along with Spieser, Hauss, Lang, Nussbaum, Schall, and Schlegel—on charges of having relations with the enemy, of committing crimes and sanctions against persons, of affiliating with criminal organizations, and of participating in the forced conscription of a country occupied by Germany. The sentence passed on Bickler was death, national indignity, and the confiscation of property. In the case of Bickler, the death warrant (*arrêt*) could not be fixed to the door of his domicile (28, rue Twinger) because the building had been destroyed by bombs during the war. And as of December 11, 1951, the arrest warrant was "still in effect [*exécutoire*]."[31]

The French pursued Hermann Bickler diligently throughout the pretrial period and after the verdict, but their efforts were to no avail. Bickler was identified at various times as being near Tübingen, in Gera in the Soviet zone, and in Italy, but he always managed to escape the French intelligence agents.[32] In 1961, a series of official interrogations of Bickler's relatives and those of his wife's established that the couple had attended a family reunion at Zweibrücken (in the Saar at Pentecost) two years earlier and that Bickler's mother-in-law, a resident of Strasbourg, knew the couple's current address.[33]

The last item in Bickler's dossier states that his death
sentence was in effect until September 30, 1967, but that
if he were apprehended before that date, the State Security Court (Cour de sûreté d'Etat) would have to decide
whether the sentence in absentia had been purged or
not. By inference, any criminal charges against Bickler
after the September 1967 date were null and void.[34]
When interviewed in Strasbourg in July 1972, Bâtonnier S. (president of the French bar) admitted that
the city's legal establishment had protected Bickler before the war, knowing that he was a "traitor." Bâtonnier
S. refused, however, to reveal Bickler's current address,
explaining, "I don't have the right."[35] So Bickler's ghost,
at least, is still present, alone among the autonomists in
Alsace.

Spieser, who had been arraigned in absentia at the
same time as Bickler, was ordered to appear in court for
trial on July 29, 1946. As a Frenchman, he was accused
of having relations with the enemy and of having borne
arms against France. He was found guilty at the same
time as the others and received the same sentence—
death, national indignity, and confiscation of property.
The *arrêt* was posted at the Hôtel de Ville in Strasbourg
and on the door of the town hall in Dossenheim-zur-
Zinsel, a hamlet near the Hünenburg (which had been
confiscated by the French on October 4, 1947).[36]

There was some attempt to locate Spieser in the
American zone, for it was known that he fled with a mass
of refugees into Thuringia, leaving his wife and family
near Darmstadt.[37] But once the verdict was handed
down and the property confiscated, his dossier reveals
no evidence of any further efforts to find him. There
is merely the pathetic case of Jeanne Flick, a maid
in the Spieser family since 1938. After being transported
by them to Schloss Wundlacken in 1939, returned in
1940, and taken with them again in their 1944 flight, she

was repatriated on July 16, 1945, from Schloss Lisch, the temporary home of Spieser's family. She immediately came to the attention of the police who thought she was an agent sent to Alsace to see what the French government was doing about her master's legal case and his valuable property. After several depositions had established her apolitical status and her kindnesses to Polish prisoners-of-war, she was released from the Struthof camp to stand trial in civil court; she was forbidden to reside in Strasbourg or its environs, in Wissembourg, and above all, in Saverne.[38] At last accounts, Spieser, who published his gigantic memoirs (really, *mémoires-fleuve*) in 1952, is living in a sort of small-scale Hünenburg near Heilbronn, Burg Stettenfels, receiving elegant (and high-paying) tourists with baronial honors. He, too, has been forgotten in today's Alsace.

6

Conclusion

After the postwar executions and prison sentences, the leaders of the interwar Alsatian autonomist movement passed into oblivion. They were bankrupt; French justice had been their fate, but their German masters (in the persons of Ernst and Wagner) had already thwarted their aims for autonomy and opened the way for the reign of terror that the Nazi occupation became. In retrospect, how mild and tolerant the prewar centralists from Paris—men like Herriot, Poincaré, Guy la Chambre, and Léon Blum—must have seemed. At least under the French, autonomist theories could be voiced openly and autonomist goals pursued until the outbreak of the war in 1939. Under the Germans, autonomism could only result in arrest, deportation, and even decapitation.

The failure of the five leaders we have studied should, by now, be amply illustrated. But in spite of this common trait, they were quite different in nature, methods, and goals. Only their incarceration together— along with a host of lesser figures—could make them into an amalgam: the *Colmariens* in 1928, the *Nanziger* in 1939 and 1940. Of the five, Joseph Rossé and Marcel Stürmel stand together as the leaders not only of the largest party in Alsace, the U.P.R., but also of the wing of autonomism that had the greatest chance of success. Their goal was administrative autonomy (or regionalism,

as Dreyfus has called it), a program that was realistic
and possible (as shown by the royalist memorandum
examined in Chapter 2). The reality of the French
Jacobin Republic *une et indivisible* should not be exag-
gerated into a myth: if the Locarno reconciliation with
Germany in the 1920s had not given way to irredentism
under Hitler during the 1930s, there was at least a
chance, and a good one, that the French eventually
would have given Alsace a special constitutional statute
akin to that granted by Germany in 1911. It is true, of
course, that under Weimar the Germans poured much
money into the Alsatian autonomist cause, but German
officials were always careful to insist that the province
remain within the French cadre, a principle maintained
even by the chief German irredentist leader, Robert
Ernst, until the Nazi victory of June 1940. But under
conditions of near-mobilization in both countries during
the 1930s, and as the Third Republic declined in both
prestige and vigor, concessions to Alsatian autonomy
from Paris became problematical, to say the least.

Unquestionably, Joseph Rossé was the most important and most forceful of the Alsatian autonomist
leaders between 1919 and 1947. It was Rossé, not
Stürmel, who inherited the mantle of leadership from
Abbé Haegy and Georges Ricklin as the pre–World War
I generation of autonomists passed from the scene during
the late 1920s. Rossé was never a separatist: the seces-
sion of the A.P.N.A. from the U.P.R. and his defeat in
1934 when he tried to lead the U.P.R. party into collaboration with the Landespartei were bitter lessons to him
and well learned. He detested the strange bedfellows
with whom he was thrown together at Colmar and
Nancy: it was he, not Roos, who was elected to represent
Alsace as a deputy to the French Chamber in 1928 and
again in 1932; it was he, not Bickler, who in 1940 objected to the surrender of the whole autonomist program

until Ernst's threats forced him to sign the Trois Epis proclamation. And, finally, it was Rossé who, when stripped of his illusions concerning neo-autonomism, had the candor to recognize the wishes of his electorate by stating that Alsace desired an administration that would allow her to retain, within the French framework, her "own patrimony, handed down by our fathers, [and] to care for [our] special interests."[1]

Rossé's relations with the Germans were curious. He accepted German money because he believed that his German friends desired for Alsace only cultural autonomy within the French cadre and the maintenance of the religious settlement. These were precisely the aims of the "clerical" German irredentists with whom Rossé had the most contact; Ernst, it will be remembered, was a relatively shadowy figure on the fringes of Rossé's political life. In retrospect, how Rossé could have avoided recognizing Hitler's *Grossdeutsch* mentality, especially as annexation succeeded annexation in central Europe during the 1930s, is puzzling indeed. But it is safe to say that Joseph Rossé was not the only one in prewar Europe to have been duped before 1940 by the führer's behavior.

As long as France and Germany remained at peace with one another and in an approximate balance of power, Rossé could maneuver and pursue his goals, year after year, gradually wearing down the opposition in Paris. But when the two countries went to war, there was no more room left to pressure and negotiate: Rossé was entirely at the mercy of the victor. And when that victor turned out to be Hitler's Germany, which paradoxically had nurtured the autonomist movement throughout the 1930s, Rossé was brutally and effectively throttled. The sad episode of his far-fetched neo-autonomism of the early occupation years shows cruelly and completely his utter powerlessness and futility. Rossé did indeed serve his German masters during the war years, but in such a manner that he brought financial benefit to Alsatians, including himself, not to the Nazis. The French postwar courts recognized Rossé's special record by condemning him to prison, not to the firing squad. Of all the autonomists it is perhaps this man who, in his coherent aims and eventual total defeat, fits most closely the classical definition of tragedy.

Marcel Stürmel, on the other hand, never attained Rossé's stature, despite his longer service in the French Chamber and, in an overall sense, his greater effectiveness there on behalf of the interests of Alsace. Part of the explanation for this lies in the fact that Stürmel was not, as Rossé was, the favorite of Abbé Haegy and never possessed the financial resources of the Alsatia publishing empire. Part of the explanation also lies in Stürmel's less impressive personal and intellectual qualities: he inherited Ricklin's seat in the Chamber but not Ricklin's leadership of the U.P.R.

There is, throughout Stürmel's career, a thread of vulgarity which was manifested in his avid grasping for power and status and in his behavior in Paris, with his electorate, and with his chief German contact, Emile Clément Scherer. Stürmel did not recognize the dangers of his prewar dealings with the Germans any more than did his distinguished colleague; for Stürmel, it was all a question of money. "Paris wouldn't give us any, so we turned to Germany" was his explanation in 1971. Certainly the same vulgarity was displayed after the Trois Epis declaration in his conduct toward the victor: he made anti-French speeches during the summer of 1940; he applied for membership in the party and the SS; and he searched frantically for a sinecure in the occupier's administration.

But Stürmel was far less fortunate than Rossé in his post under the Nazis: he was in direct contact with the German occupiers in Mulhouse, Alsace's second major Kreisleitung. Stürmel had a particularly heavy burden to balance, especially as the prewar representative from the Sundgau, scene of the Ballersdorf massacre and the most active anti-German area in all of Alsace. There is, as has been indicated, evidence that Stürmel acquitted himself honorably under the circumstances, although he was distrusted by Germans and Alsatians alike. Like Rossé, he was a man without a cause after the Trois Epis manifesto. Again, this fact was recognized by the French courts after the liberation; he was condemned to hard labor, not death. Certainly it was ironic that Stürmel survived Rossé by twenty years, becoming the only autonomist leader to return to his native town and finally to lead a comfortable, even complacent, existence. What his papers contain is anyone's guess; Stürmel boasted to me in 1971 that he was writing the history of the entire autonomist movement. One might only suppose that in his account, Stürmel will not assign himself the secondary role that was his fate.

Jean-Pierre Mourer was the authentic voice of the proletariat in the interwar autonomist movement. The impression he made in Frankfurt in 1923—brawny, strapping, and vociferous—upon Robert Ernst, the bourgeois son of a pastor and a graduate student in philology, was of tremendous importance. Mourer was, throughout, the faithful servant of his Strasbourg electorate, most of whom had migrated since the end of the First World War from the Lutheran, German-speaking separatist communes along the Palatinate border to the city's suburbs. Mourer braved the intricate twists and turns of the French Communist party: first, it forbade his liaisons with bourgeois autonomist parties, and then it banned autonomism altogether as Stalin allied himself in 1934 and 1935 with the western bourgeois democracies, in-

cluding France. Despite his exclusion from the national
organization on both counts of deviation from the party
line, Mourer remained a steadfast autonomist and a
Communist through three elections before the beginning
of the Second World War.

Mourer was certainly more realistic and cold-
blooded in his dealings with the "secular" German irredentists. He knew that his chances of survival in
dealing with the Third Reich lay not in the latter's last-
minute willingness to compromise with Stalinist Russia,
but in his own ability to nationalize—in this case, "auton-
omize"—his brand of communism. How else could the
Sicherheitsdienst or the Gestapo have permitted Ernst
to use Mourer as peacemaker in the jungle politics of
secular autonomism during the 1930s? How else could
Mourer, at the end of the decade, dream of becoming
(through his manipulation of Roos) the chief of secular
autonomism in Bas-Rhin?

That Mourer knew his "workers' autonomism" was
a sham is evidenced by his behavior in prison at Nancy
in 1939 and 1940. But his attempt to cajole French
justice into handing down a verdict of mercy for him led
only to his desperate quandry during the summer of
1940, when he believed he was on the Gestapo's "hunted"
list because of Bickler's and Schall's denunciations. From
here, it was but one step further into the fire: because
of his "proletarian" appeal, Mourer was offered the
Kreisleitung of Mulhouse. He grasped at the offer as a
way to escape his tormentors—a fatal decision as it
turned out. In Mulhouse, Mourer—like the other autonomist leaders, now a rebel without a cause—lost his
always tenuous links with reality. Under the influence of
drink and excess in all aspects of his life, Mourer became
a character straight out of the inferno of Nazi politics:
he and Erich Koch, the Gauleiter of East Prussia, at the
opposite end of Hitler's empire, had much in common.

When morning dawned, there were few to testify in
Mourer's favor: he became the only one of the leaders
to pay with his life for the once-brilliant dream of an
autonomous Alsace, with which at one time he had en-
thralled his working-class audiences.

Hermann (Armand) Bickler was the leader of the
younger, more extremist generation of interwar autonomists. It can be said of Bickler that had he not existed,
he would have been invented, so inevitable was the
appearance of a figure like him in the autonomist movement of the 1930s. Bickler was typical of Europe during
that decade with his fascistic Jungmannschaft, his rhetoric, and his separatist aims. He was the Konrad Henlein
of Alsace, paradoxically protected by his fellow lawyers
in the Strasbourg bar from the consequences of his
treasonous activities; he was an authentic Alsatian Nazi.
In contrast to the others (even Spieser—at least until
the Munich crisis of 1938), Bickler desired more than
autonomy or even separatism. He coldly and cynically
envisioned Alsace's annexation by Nazi Germany; his
publicly voiced support for autonomy and separatism
was a facade, a front for his dreams of devolution to the
Reich.

Although Bickler appealed to autonomist radicals
on both the political and the social level, neither his own
Jungmannschaft nor certainly the Landespartei, which
he was bent on absorbing, would have accepted his be-
trayal of autonomism. The German irredentists with
whom he had had close connections would also have
been shocked at Bickler's *Grossdeutsch* mentality during
the 1930s—especially Ernst who was careful always to
play this *petit avocat* ("petty lawyer") and would-be
führer off agaist Mourer. Bickler's espionage for the
Sicherheitsdienst during the decade pulled him in the
direction of reunion with Germany; his efforts to lead a
united front of the Jungmannschaft, Landespartei, and

Communist Autonomists diverted him temporarily from his aim of incorporating Alsace into the Reich. In his attempt to turn state's evidence at Nancy in April 1940, Bickler, always the opportunist, showed himself to be not only eager to escape Karl Roos's fate, execution, but also aware that his autonomist constituency would never accept the German annexation he dreamed of. It is this point, perhaps, which should be emphasized, rather than Bickler's abject grovelling at the feet of the German conquerors at Trois Epis in July 1940.

Ernst and Wagner recognized Bickler's special status within the ranks of the *Nanziger* by appointing him to the chief Kreisleitung in Alsace, Strasbourg. They were convinced that he would wage the most energetic campaign of any autonomist leader to integrate Alsace into Nazi Germany. Neither Wagner nor Ernst was disappointed in Bickler's performance as Kreisleiter, but they misunderstood completely the ambition and strong sense of self-preservation of their protégé. With the connivance of his Sicherheitsdienst friends, Bickler made good his escape as an *embusqué* ("rear-sector soldier") from the terrors of the eastern front to the delights of Paris in early 1943. The talents he then developed to maintain himself in this safe haven until the end of the war served him well after Germany's defeat. In eluding the French police after 1945, most certainly aided by his old Sicherheitsdienst friends, Bickler escaped execution, the fate that would certainly have been his at the hands of the postwar French courts. But the cost was a kind of living death for one who, publicly at least, had exalted Alsace above both France and Germany to his enthusiastic prewar autonomist followers. Bickler has not seen the *Heimat* for the last thirty-three years; he is still hunted, still in exile.

Friedrich Spieser was also of the younger generation of autonomist leaders and of separatist rather than autonomist leanings. Although Ernst's protégé from the very start of his career, Spieser was much more strongly affected than his master by the annexationist fever that so seduced Bickler (who was Spieser's first contact when he returned to Alsace in 1931). It was possible for Spieser to avoid Bickler's vacillations over the issue of reunion with Germany, for he had no autonomist constituency to satisfy other than the Hünenburg's guests, who were only to be persuaded that Alsace had unique cultural characteristics. But it is true that as the 1930s progressed, Spieser's increased emphasis on the "Germanic" content of this heritage pushed him far into the annexationist camp; by the outbreak of the war, he had far outdistanced his mentor, Ernst, his secret Maecenas, Alfred Toepfer, and even the Reich chancellery itself. He was, by that time, much more radical in his solution of the Alsatian "problem" than any of the others, as illustrated by the fate of his letter to the führer in September 1939, calling for annexation of Alsace by the Reich.

The triumph of Spieser's return to Alsace in the baggage-train of the victorious Wehrmacht in June 1940 was brief indeed. The region's new masters, Wagner and Ernst, did not trust Spieser's administrative or political abilities sufficiently to give him more than cultural duties in the new occupation. Worse still was the fact that Spieser's cherished Hünenburg, built with so much guile and money, was now superfluous: it was no longer the famous outpost in a foreign land; Alsace was German again. Even Spieser's political loyalty was suspect, in part because his 1939 appeal to the führer had not been signed *"Heil Hitler"* but *"Long Live the Reich"*[2] and in part because he was connected by marriage with the Junker aristocracy distrusted by the Nazis as reactionary and subversive. He was not admitted into the ranks of the party until long after the victory of 1940. Even more galling was the fact that the new administration left

Spieser to the mercy of an implacable enemy of annexationists, Joseph Rossé of the Indemnification Bureau. Spieser received far less monetary compensation for his prewar subversion than he felt he was entitled to as an outstanding "pioneer of Germanism." Under the circumstances, it is not surprising that Spieser, who was kept away from the mainstream of power in the German administration of Alsace (he was not even a *Nanziger*), should become secretly and then overtly rebellious, attacking the Gauleiter in his publications, contacting Rossé's neo-autonomists, and enlarging the Hünenburg despite a lack of official encouragement. It is paradoxical, to say the least, that the German occupation made an autonomist out of Spieser, formerly a fervent annexationist. This late conversion to the cause of all the other autonomist leaders (except Bickler) could not, of course, erase his prewar record by which the courts of the liberation would judge him. Like Bickler, he escaped the French police after 1945; but unlike Bickler (because he had no blood on his hands), Spieser was not pursued diligently by the authorities.

Allowing Spieser to remain free in exile in Germany may have been the best punishment that French justice could have meted out. Rather than enjoying prolonged distraction in a legal defense, Spieser has been condemned to a life of reflecting on how the Germans blasted his cleverly concealed, ardently pursued, prewar annexationist dreams. His fate has been, perhaps, the most ignominious of all the leaders': he has been for a generation, and will remain forever, merely a decorative figure, tormented by his memory of deserting the cause as the chatelain of the Hünenburg during the 1930s.

At first glance, the thesis of this study—namely, that the interwar Alsatian autonomist leaders were failures

and that by 1947 their movement was reduced to ashes
—would seem to be disproved by a recent manifesto.
Issued on November 15, 1970, by a professional man of
Bas-Rhin, Dr. Marcel Iffrig, on behalf of the Alsace-
Lorraine Regionalist Movement, it contains eerie remi-
niscences of the Heimatbund document of some forty-
four years earlier:

> Responsible Alsace-Lorrainers . . . have decided to
> group themselves in a popular union to denounce this
> colonial situation [under France], and to defend
> threatened interests. . . . Our objectives: [a] Constitu-
> tion, within the French framework, . . . an Alsace-
> Lorraine territorial entity . . . [with] a Regional Parlia-
> ment, . . . an Economic, Social, and Cultural Council,
> . . . [and] a Regional Executive. . . .[3]

This manifesto was greeted with an angry denunciation
by the Gaullist representatives of Alsace in the French
Chamber, who issued a proclamation saying,

> this enterprise must be excoriated, for we know what
> similar movements before the Second World War led
> our eastern provinces to. . . . Indifference and forgetful-
> ness [of the past] must reinforce the shame of those who
> have committed this gesture.[4]

At approximately the same time, signs of revived
German interest in the former Reichsland began to
appear. For example, purchase of the ancient and
historical Château de Kientzheim in Haut-Rhin by German interests in 1972 was avoided only by a national
subscription undertaken by the Confrérie Saint-Etienne,
Alsace's version of the Chevaliers du Tastevin. In addition, there was increasing activity of the Alsatian-
Franco-German Cercle René Schickelé, founded in honor
of a bilingual Alsatian poet and *littérateur* who spent
most of his life in Germany; "We wish to keep our
language" was the theme of its pamphleteering.[5] Still

another sign was the founding, during the summer of
1975 in the Münster valley (Haut-Rhin), of a Hünen-
burg-like youth center called the Alsatian University,
under the auspices of the Alsace-Lorraine Regionalist
Movement. And on May 18, 1975, the EL-Front Autonomiste de Libération, a youth movement pledged to the
preservation of Alsatian "liberties" and its ecology, was
created. It joined the Permanent Office of European
Nations without a State in Brussels in June 1975; one of
its leaders, Ferdinand Moschenross, won 11 percent of
the votes in the Alsatian cantonal elections the following
March.[6]

Is there a connection between these events, these
groups, and the interwar autonomist and irredentist
activities? In the last analysis, such a tie seems superficial, despite the language of recent autonomism and
regionalism. The German versions of two tracts issued
by Dr. Iffrig, for example, are openly provocative. *Elsa*,
the movement's periodical, states: "If our language and
our customs do not please the French of the Interior,
then they should go home. We did not summon them
here and do very well without them."[7] And a broadside
for a meeting in Guebwiller (Haut-Rhin) asserts that:

> In spite of Liberty, Equality, Fraternity, our Alsace-
> Lorraine is culturally exterminated, economically under-
> developed, financially plundered. Strangers and carpet-
> baggers lord it over us.
>
> So that we can be lord and master in our own land,
> E-L. fights and invites you to an open meeting. Bring
> your friends. Free discussion.[8]

One of the moving forces behind the attempted
German purchase of the Château de Kientzheim in 1972
were the irrepressible Toepfer brothers of Hamburg; and
the new Münster University also was rumored to have
been supported by German funds. In July 1975, the

EL-Front Autonomiste de Libération plastered the town of Turckheim (Haut-Rhin) with posters on the three-hundredth anniversary of the death of Louis XIV's great marshal, Henri de la Tour d'Auvergne, vîcomte de Turenne, denouncing him as the "hangman and incendiary" of the old city.[9] Finally, at the end of 1976 Paul Schall, a minor interwar autonomist and editor of the German-dominated *Strassburger Neueste Nachrichten* during the occupation, published a stinging rebuke to Lothar Kettenacker's *Nationalsozialistische Volkstumspolitik im Elsass.* (Kettenacker's book was published by the prestigious Institut für Zeitgeschichte in Munich; Schall's by the German organization most active in keeping the myth of German Alsace alive today, the Erwin von Steinbach Stiftung.) Schall, condemned to death in absentia by the French courts and currently living in Germany, staunchly defended the actions of the pre-1947 autonomists without, however, mentioning their specific dealings with sympathetic German personalities and organizations. Using Ernst's memoirs, Schall also justified the policy and actions of Wagner during the occupation. He ended his book with a four-page attack by a resuscitated Bickler on Robert Heitz, resistance hero and postwar councillor of Strasbourg.[10]

Despite the presence of familiar phraseology and figures, today's autonomism is independent of the interwar movement; tremendous changes have taken place since the Second World War. There has been the French government's adoption of regionalism and decentralization in various forms, and its current vogue in French political circles;[11] the postwar reconciliation between France and Germany; and the shock waves of unrest and strikes in 1968 which caused Paris to look at Alsace with new interest and solicitude.[12] All of these factors make the current autonomist movement a new phenomenon, taking place within a European context entirely different from that of the interwar years.

What the fate of the new autonomists will be is, of course, pure speculation. It will undoubtedly be different from the destiny of the older leaders, all of whom failed in some way or other: Rossé and Stürmel in their administrative autonomy, Mourer in his political autonomy, Bickler in his separatism, and Spieser in his annexationism. But their collective failure was not entirely without positive results: it taught the Alsatians the pricelessness of political freedom, and the Germans, the total vanity of forcible military solutions to complex political and social problems. If one defines nationality as based on a group's subjective identification of its own destiny,[13] then the Alsatians are permanently French. And if Alsace, while maintaining her individuality,[14] can become another bridge between contemporary France and Germany, then the failure of her interwar autonomist leaders will be transformed into the fulfillment of the region's ancient historical and geographical role in European life.

Notes

CHAPTER 1

1. J-J. Hatt, "La préhistoire" and "L'Alsace romaine"; Philippe Dollinger, "Du royaume franc au Saint-Empire," in Philippe Dollinger, ed., *Histoire de l'Alsace* (Toulouse, 1970), pp. 11–62.
2. See Anthony D. Smith, *Theories of Nationalism* (London, 1971), pp. 172–73, 214.
3. "Province à l'instar de l'étranger effectif." G. Livet, "Le 18e. siècle et l'esprit des lumières," in Dollinger, *Histoire*, p. 320; for the medieval and Renaissance periods, see Philippe Dollinger, "Le déclin du moyen âge," and F. Rapp, "Discipline et prospérité (1530–1618)," in ibid., pp. 144, 220–22.
4. R. Marx, "De la pré-révolution à la restauration," ibid., p. 357; for the quotation, see Franklin Ford, *Strasbourg in Transition, 1648–1789* (Cambridge, Mass., 1958), pp. 259–62, 264.
5. Saint-Marc Girardin, cited in Fernand L'Huillier, "L'évolution dans la paix (1814–1870)," in Dollinger, *Histoire*, p. 424. In fact, the pre-1919 records of the *état civil* of the commune of Mittelbergheim (Bas-Rhin), where the research for this study was done, were written in French only after 1804; the first French inscription in the handwritten registers appears on July 14, 1790, the date of the Fête de la Fédération in Paris (Fr. Meiss, former registrar of the commune of Mittelbergheim, to the author, December 16, 1974).
6. See Dan P. Silverman, *Reluctant Union: Alsace-Lorraine and Imperial Germany, 1871–1918* (University Park, Pa., 1972), pp. 27–28.

7. Fernand L'Huillier, "L'Alsace dans le Reichsland (1871–1918)," in Dollinger, *Histoire*, p. 436.

8. Ibid., p. 437.

9. Ibid., p. 440; see also, Johann Schneider, *Die Elsässische Autonomistenpartei, 1871–1881* (Frankfurt-am-Main, 1933), pp. 18, 94, 115.

10. L'Huillier, "Reichsland," p. 439.

11. Koppel Pinson, *Modern Germany: Its History and Civilization* (New York, 1954), p. 158.

12. L'Huillier, "Reichsland," pp. 451–52, 458.

13. Ibid., p. 454; Silverman, *Union*, pp. 133–48.

14. The leading authority on the constitutional bill, Jean-Marie Mayeur, supports this point in his *Autonomie et politique en Alsace: la constitution de 1911* (Paris, 1970), p. 114; also concurring are L'Huillier, "Reichsland," pp. 453–54, and Silverman, *Union*, p. 149.

15. L'Huillier, "Reichsland," p. 455.

16. Interview, December 1, 1974, with Alfred Heyler, son of Théophile Heyler; see Alsace, *Zweite Kammer des Landtags, 31 Sitzung am 7 Mai, 1912* (Strasbourg, 1912), pp. 1760–1837.

17. See L'Huillier, "Reichsland," pp. 457–58; Silverman, *Union*, pp. 190–92. The Alsatian was Graf Hugo Zorn von Bulach.

18. Frederic H. Seager, "The Alsace-Lorraine Question in France, 1871–1914," in Charles K. Warner, ed., *From the Ancien Régime to the Popular Front: Essays in the History of Modern France in Honor of Shepard B. Clough* (New York, 1969), p. 126; cf. John C. Cairns, "International Politics and the Military Mind: The Case of the French Republic, 1911–1914," *Journal of Modern History* 25 (September 1953): 281, 285.

19. Jean-Paul Sartre, *Les mots* (Paris, 1964), p. 129; Sartre's maternal grandfather was the uncle of the most famous twentieth-century Alsatian, Albert Schweitzer.

20. Charles Spindler, *L'Alsace pendant la guerre* (Strasbourg, 1925), pp. 86–87; L'Huillier, "Reichsland," p. 462.

21. L'Huillier, "Reichsland," p. 464; see Hans W. Gatzke, *Germany's Drive to the West (Drang nach Westen)* (Baltimore, 1950), pp. 30, 221, 234, 275, 288. Dallwitz's report of

December 19, 1917, is quoted in L'Huillier, "Reichsland," p. 463.
22. Silverman, *Union*, p. 199.
23. Spindler, *L'Alsace*, p. 759 (entry for February 4, 1919).

CHAPTER 2

1. See the reaction of Anselmne Laugel, Charles Spindler's friend and a participant in the Conférence d'Alsace et de Lorraine which had been meeting in Paris since 1915, in Spindler, *L'Alsace*, p. 744 (entry for December 4, 1918).
2. *Le Temps*, April 17, 1929, p. 3. For the records of these commissions, see France, Archives du Bas-Rhin (Strasbourg), No. AL 140, Bordereau des dossiers provenant du Commissariat Général de la République à Strasbourg et de la Haute-Commission interalliée des territoires rhénans, 1919-1939 [hereafter cited as Arch. B-R., No. AL 140], paquet 8, vol. 53 (Expulsions), vol. 54 (Projet d'un fichier des expulsés), vol. 43 (Permis ou interdictions de séjour; demandes de séjour; demandes d'évacuation).
3. The posters for the rally, all in dialect, are signed by 's Comité von dr Union démocratique nationale d'Alsace-Lorraine. See France, Archives du Bas-Rhin (Strasbourg), No. AL 98, Verzeichnis der "Valot-Akten" (Direction générale des services d'Alsace-Lorraine à Paris) [hereafter cited as Arch. B-R., No. AL 98], paquet 7, vol. 39 (Commissariat général de la République à Strasbourg, Police politique, Expulsions, élargissements, Police des étrangers . . . [1918-1919]), pièce 143.
4. Arch. B-R., No. AL 140, paquet 8 (Commissariat général de la République à Strasbourg, Enquêtes de police administrative ou politique [novembre, 1918-novembre, 1919] . . . extraits de dossiers des services d'espionnage et de contre-espionnage), vol. 50, no pièce number; vol. 44, pièce 124.
5. France, Archives du Haut-Rhin (Colmar), Cour d'appel de Colmar, Le procès des autonomistes [hereafter cited as Arch. H-R., Procès des autonomistes], cote 35791, perquisition du *Courrier d'Alsace (Elsässer Kurier)* à Colmar, various documents.

6. The "madman" description comes from René Schlegel, later secretary of the Heimatbund and Bulach's associate in the Landespartei. See note 17, this chapter, and Arch. H-R., Procès des autonomistes, cote 35793, inculpés, détenus, sous-cote 11, Schlegel, René, Affaire 173/27, procès-verbal d'interrogatoire de l'inculpé . . . le 17 février, 1928, p. 4. The French evaluation is taken from an undated and unnumbered report (probably compiled in 1922) in Arch. B-R., No. AL 140, paquet 8, vol. 52, Zorn von Bulach; brochure in ibid.

7. The Cour d'Assises du Bas-Rhin on May 15, 1920 condemned Ley, Muth, and Rapp to life deportation (see also note 20, this chapter); Arch. B-R., No. AL 140, paquet 8, vol. 52, Zorn von Bulach.

8. Harry Paul, *The Second Ralliement: The Rapprochement between Church and State in France in the Twentieth Century* (Washington, D.C., 1967), pp. 122–25; this account also refers to the actions of Mgr. Charles Ruch, archbishop of Strasbourg, at the time. The best analysis in French of this struggle is found in François G. Dreyfus, *La vie politique en Alsace, 1919–1936* (Paris, 1969), pp. 56–69, 81–90. Herriot's memoirs do not mention the Alsatian side of the crisis; see *Jadis*, vol. 2, *D'une guerre à l'autre, 1914–1936* (Paris, 1952), pp. 226–33.

9. Dreyfus, *Vie politique*, pp. 97–98.

10. Mourer later boasted of these demands in a vita given the Nazis while he was serving as *Kreisleiter* ("district leader") of Mulhouse during the German occupation of Alsace. See France, Ministère de la Justice, Cour de justice du Haut-Rhin, sous-section de Mulhouse, Chambre d'instruction no. 4, P.C. 43/67 (Archives du Haut-Rhin, Colmar, cote 34127), Procès de Mourer, Jean-Pierre, 49 ans, ex-Kreisleiter de Mulhouse [hereafter cited as Justice, Procès Mourer], III, Pièces d'information, chemise no. 4 (Activité de Mourer comme Kreisleiter), An den Gaupersonalamtsleiter des NSDAP Pg. Schuppel, 25 Februar, 1941, cote 4, C-4, p. 33, C-13.

11. Arch. H-R., Procès des autonomistes, cote 35793, inculpés, détenus, sous-cote 10, Schall, Paul, procès-verbal d'interrogatoire de l'inculpé . . . le 23–24 février, 1928, p. 1. The

other Schall publication involved in the courts was *D'Stadt-brill*, which enjoyed only a brief existence during 1919.

12. France, Ministère d' Etat chargé des Affaires culturelles, Archives nationales, Section moderne, F⁷, Police générale, Direction des renseignements généraux, III, Alsace-Lorraine, cote 13400, liasse no. 2 [hereafter cited as Arch. nat., F⁷ 13400], Le Commissaire spécial à M. le Directeur des services généraux de police et d'Alsace-Lorraine, no. 1935, le 23 décembre, 1925, pièce 1028, p. 17. For the aborted parliamentary bills, see note 18, this chapter, and Dreyfus, *Vie politique*, pp. 102, 112–13. The calculation of the *Zukunft's* readership is in ibid., p. 94.

13. Reprinted in *La voix d'Alsace* 7, no. 8 (February 20, 1926): 1–2.

14. Arch. B-R., No. AL 98, paquet 1283, vol. 28, Rapports des préfets . . . Préfecture du Haut-Rhin, Cabinet, à M. le Sous-secrétaire d'Etat à la Présidence du Conseil (Direction des services d'Alsace-Lorraine), le 7 janvier, 1926, confidentiel.

15. Arch. H-R., Procès des autonomistes, cote 35792, le 5 juin, 1926.

16. René Hauss's account of the meeting, held May 24, 1926, which prepared the manifesto is the most complete; Rossé's version is the fullest from the U.P.R. point of view. Ibid., cote 35793 . . . sous-cote 4 . . . procès-verbal d'interrogatoire de l'inculpé, Hauss, René, le 21 et 22 février, 1928, pp. 4–6; sous-cote 9 . . . procès-verbal d'interrogatoire de l'inculpé Rossé, Joseph, le 23 mars, 1928, pp. 1–2.

17. Ibid., sous-cote 10 . . . procès-verbal d'interrogatoire de l'inculpé Schall, Paul, le 23–24 février, 1928, pp. 8–15. Of interest also is Hauss's description of the negotiations with Bulach leading to the formation of the Landespartei in November 1927; see ibid., sous-cote 4 . . . procès-verbal d'interrogatoire de l'inculpé Hauss, René, le 21–22 février, 1928, pp. 4–6.

18. For the first bill, which was never reported out of the Commission [sic] de l'administration générale, départementale, et communale, see France, *Journal officiel de la république française, Sénat, 1876–1940: Débats parlementaires,*

Compte rendu in extenso, 11 janvier 1881–21 mai 1940 (Paris, 1881–1940) [hereafter cited as *J. O. S. Débs.*], le 5 août, 1926, p. 1491; for the Painlevé, Poincaré, and Daladier visits, see Dreyfus, *Vie politique*, pp. 98, 107, 145.

19. France, Ministère d'Etat chargé de la Défense nationale, Direction de la Gendarmerie et de la justice militaire, Justice militaire, Dépôt central des archives, Caserne Noëfort (Meaux), Tribunal permanent des Forces Armées de Metz, Inventaire des pièces de la procédure suivie contre le nommé Ernst, Robert Frédéric . . . [hereafter cited as Déf. nat., Procès Ernst], liasse no. 2 (Instruction, 2e. partie), rapport signé Ernst à Metz, le 7 août, 1947, cote 494, pp. 1–2.

20. Germany, Auswärtiges Amt, Politisches Archiv, Geheimakten 1920–1936, Länder II, Frankreich, Politik 5, Elsass-Lothringen: Die Stellung Elsass-Lothringen im französischen Staat, sowie die Elsass-Lothringische Autonomiefrage, Band 1 [hereafter cited as Aus. Amt, Geheimakten, Fr.], Abschrift zu Nr. II, Fr. 3689, Karlsruhe, den 4 Mai, 1921; das Auswärtiges Amt an die deutsche Botschaft in Paris, Nr. II, Fr. 793, den 28 Februar, 1925. See also, U.S. National Archives, Series T-120 [hereafter cited as T-120], serial 2804, frame E439302 (Berlin, den 4 Februar, 1925).

21. Ernst to Dr. von Loesch, in Déf. nat., Procès Ernst, liasse no. 1 (Instruction, 1ère partie), procès-verbal d'interrogatoire ou de confrontation du nommé Ernst, Robert, le 21 février, 1947, cote 31, pp. 1–4; see a letter to Ernst from the newspaper's chief editor, Ernst Breisacher, in ibid., cote 17.

22. Ernst portrays himself as the chief supporter of the Alsatian autonomists in a letter to Dr. Östreich, chief editor of the *Berliner Börsenzeitung*, ibid., cotes 15–16.

23. See undated letter written during the Nazi occupation of Alsace from Fasshauer to Rossé in ibid., cote 41.

24. Ibid., liasse no. 1, procès-verbal d'interrogatoire ou de confrontation, du nommé Ernst, Robert, le 4 mars, 1947, cote 32, p. 2; le 6 mars, 1947, cote 36, pp. 2–3.

25. Ibid., liasse no. 2, Rapport signé Ernst à Metz, le 7 août, 1947, cote 494, p. 4.

26. The record of the meeting and the legal documents of the transfer of funds are all found in ibid., liasse no. 1, procès-

verbal d'interrogatoire ou de confrontation du nommé Ernst, Robert, le 25 octobre, 1946, cote 29, pp. 3–4, 5; cotes 34–35.
27. Aus. Amt, Geheimakten, Fr., Politische Abteilung II, Elsass-Lothringen, Politik 26, Politische und kulturelle Propaganda, Band 1, Das Auswärtiges Amt an den Herrn Ministerialdirektor Goetz . . . den 18 Mai, 1921, Nr. II, Fr. 2960; Unterrichtsministerium an Herrn Ministeralrat von Seydewitz, den 21 Februar, 1925, Nr. II, Fr. 4575.
28. The *Zukunft* matter is reviewed in T-120/2804, E439308–11 (den 20 April, 1925), E439312 (den 11 August, 1925), E439313 (den 12 August, 1925). The 280,000RM subsidy figure (T-120/2277/E134044 [den 5 April, 1930]) is an average for the period from 1927 to 1929; it is contradicted by an earlier total for 1927 of 600,000RM, payable in four quarterly installments (T-120/2277/E133925 [den 28 Juni, 1927]).
29. T-120/2277/E133913 (undated); Gustav Stresemann, *Vermächtnis, der Nachlass* . . . 2 vols. (Berlin, 1932–33), 2: 115, 125, 139, 553.
30. France, Ministère de la Justice, Cour de justice du Haut-Rhin, sous-section de Mulhouse, Tribunal de première instance de Mulhouse . . . Archives du Haut-Rhin (Colmar), cote des archives 34131, Procès de Stürmel, Marcel René [hereafter cited as Justice, Procès Stürmel], dossier no. 1, III (Pièces d'information), le Contrôleur général de surveillance du territoire, circonscription régional de Strasbourg, no. 14646, le 4 septembre, 1939, cote 36 (secret) (Rapport Becker).
31. The interviews took place on August 25 and September 28, 1926; Déf. nat., Procès Ernst, liasse no. 1, Rapport d'ensemble des pièces 87 à 94 adressé par le Commissaire divisionnaire des renseignements généraux à Strasbourg à M. le Commissaire du Gouvernement près la Cour de justice du Haut-Rhin, no. 4722, cote 97, pp. 3, 7.
32. For differing reports of this meeting (one from a "very good source, a good agent"), see Arch. B-R., No. AL 98, paquet 689, vol. HI-142, folder no. 1, Préfecture du Bas-Rhin, no. 1029, E. M. G., no. 76/11, Renseignement, le 17 mars, 1926; no. 1756, S. C. R. 2/11, secret, le 22 mars, 1926; folder no. 4,

Le Préfet du Bas-Rhin à M. le Garde des Sceaux, le 11 juin, 1926.

33. Alain Déniel, *Le mouvement breton, 1919–1945* (Paris, 1976), pp. 92–93; the manifesto of the Comité central des minorités is reprinted in part. See also, the memoirs of Olier Mordrel, leader of the Breton movement, *Breiz Atao, ou l'histoire et l'actualité du nationalisme breton* (Paris, 1973), pp. 135–36; and an official report on Breton-Alsatian contacts between 1927 and 1934 in Arch. B-R., No. AL 98, paquet 670, vol. HI-63, Ministère de l'Intérieur à M. le Directeur de la Sûreté générale, no. 7407, le 15 octobre, 1934, pp. 1–2.

34. Arch. B-R., No. AL 98, paquet 691, vol. HI-155, Le Commissariat spécial des ponts du Rhin et du port de Strasbourg, no. R1434, à M. le Directeur des services généraux de police d'Alsace et de Lorraine, le 10 novembre, 1927.

35. "An Autonomist Defeat in Colmar," *Le Journal d'Alsace et de Lorraine* 232 (August 23, 1926): 1–2, in Arch. nat., F⁷13400, pièces 834–44.

36. Arch. H-R., Procès des autonomistes, cote 35793, sous-cote 10, procès-verbal d'interrogatoire de l'inculpé Schall, Paul, le 23–24 février, 1928, p. 5.

37. Dreyfus, *Vie politique,* pp. 103–4, 141–42.

38. Arch. nat., F⁷13400, Rapport du Commissaire spécial à M. le Préfet du Bas-Rhin, no. 1835, le 12 octobre, 1926, pièce 671; for Rossé, see his testimony in Arch. H-R., Procès des autonomistes, cote 35793, sous-cote 9, procès-verbal d'interrogatoire de l'inculpé Rossé, Joseph, le 23 mars, 1928, pp. 1–2.

39. See the official report in the F⁷13400 series cited in note 38, this chapter; Arch. B-R., No. AL 98, paquet 675, vol. HI-83 (Les catholiques et les autonomistes), Le Commissaire spécial, Gare de Strasbourg, à M. le Directeur de la Sûreté générale, no. 1379, le 17 septembre, 1929.

40. Arch. B-R., No. AL 98, paquet 675, vol. HI-83, le Ministre des Affaires-Etrangères à M. le Président du Conseil, no. 44, le 2 avril, 1927; M. de Fontenoy, Ambassadeur de la République française près le Saint-Siège, à M. le Ministre des Affaires-Etrangères, no. 83, le 15 juin, 1928.

41. Haegy to the Colmar lawyer, Fernand-Joseph Heitz, May 27, 1931, in France, Archives du Haut-Rhin (Colmar), Collection Fernand-Joseph Heitz [hereafter cited as Arch. H-R., Coll. Heitz], cote 2J 213 36.

42. The list of those arrested, both those taken into custody and those in flight, is found in *Le procès du complot autonomiste de Colmar 1-24 mai, 1928: comptes-rendus des débats (Où est le complot?)* (Colmar, 1928) [hereafter cited as *Procès Colmar*], pp. 4-11.

43. See the letter of M. le Procureur Général près le Cour d'Appel de Colmar, no. M33-784/71 M.W., dated July 29, 1971.

44. Testimony of Joseph Fasshauer (May 8 and 9, 1928) and of Ricklin (May 15 and 24, 1928), *Procès Colmar*, pp. 61, 71, 126, 232. (Hermann Roechling's name is mentioned on p. 203.)

45. Déf. nat., Procès Ernst, liasse no. 2, Rapport signé Ernst à Metz, le 7 août, 1947, cote 494, p. 4.

46. Arch. H-R., Procès des autonomistes, cote 35792, sous-cote 10 . . . procès-verbal d'interrogatoire de l'inculpé Schall, Paul, le 23-24 février, 1928, pp. 14-15; procès-verbal d'interrogatoire de l'inculpé Rossé, Joseph, le 23 mars, 1928, pp. 1-2; testimony of Ricklin (May 24, 1928), *Procès Colmar*, pp. 232, 235, 239.

47. France, *Journal officiel de la république française 1870-1940, Chambre des députés 1876-1940: Débats parlementaires, compte rendu in extenso, 11 janvier, 1881-4 juin, 1940* (Paris, 1881-1940) [hereafter cited as *J. O. C. Débs.*], le 8 novembre, 1928, pp. 2520-25; for the regular and special elections, see Dreyfus, *Vie politique*, pp. 125, 140-42.

48. France, Ministère da la Justice, Archives départementales de Meurthe-et-Moselle (Nancy), Dossier contre Rossé, Joseph Victor, Dossier de Nancy, liasse no. I (Information devant le Tribunal militaire jusqu'en juin, 1940) [hereafter cited as Justice, M-et-M., Dossier de Nancy or Justice, M-et-M., Dossier Rossé], le Contrôleur général des services de police d'Alsace et de Lorraine à M. le Directeur général de la Sûreté nationale, no. 973, le 20 janvier, 1938, cote C-1.

49. Rossé was later accused by the government of having bribed

the head juror to secure Roos's acquittal. See ibid., Dossier Rossé, procès-verbal d'interrogatoire ou de confrontation du nommé Rossé, Joseph, le 23 novembre, 1939, cote C-21, pp. 2–3. Roos had returned from exile to attend a meeting organized by the Communist Autonomists and the U.P.R. in Strasbourg on November 9, 1928, and gave himself up to the authorities the following day.

50. Arch. H-R., Procès des autonomistes, cote 35793, sous-cote 3, procès-verbal d'interrogatoire de l'inculpé Fasshauer, Joseph, le 27 mars, 1928, p. 6; the manifesto was printed in the *National-Zeitung* (Basel), January 18, 1928 (signed also by Hirtzel and Pinck), cited in Arch. H-R., Procès des autonomistes, cote 37793, sous-cote 3, Ministère de l'intérieur, Sûreté générale, no. 469, le 23 janvier, 1928.

51. Maurice Thorez, *Oeuvres*, 23 vols. (Paris, 1950–65), 2: 154 (emphasis in original); Dreyfus, *Vie politique*, pp. 103–4, 141–42.

52. Dreyfus, *Vie politique*, p. 194.

53. T-120/2277/E134066 (den 5 April, 1930); E134068 (den 15 April, 1930).

54. Arch. B-R., No. AL 98, paquet 670, vol. HI-62 (Polizeiberichte über Dargestellten des Autonomisten), Le Commissaire spécial, la Gare de Strasbourg à M. le Préfet du Bas-Rhin, no. 1130 and 1132, le 5 mai, 1930, pp. 1–2. (This folder contains an entire series of secret reports of the monthly Landespartei meetings at the time.)

55. Ibid., paquet 674, vol. HI-79 (U.P.R., 1933–1934), Le Controleur général à M. le Directeur général de la Sûreté nationale, no. 4955, le 13 juin, 1934, pp. 1–2. This was interpreted as a victory of the U.P.R.'s right wing (i.e., Michel Walter, Meck, Seltz, Brogly, and Brom) over its left wing (i.e., Stürmel, Rossé, Gromer, and Keppi).

56. Dreyfus, *Vie politique*, p. 270; Réquisitoire du Procureur Général (May 21, 1928), *Procès Colmar*, p. 177.

57. The 1931 project of the U.P.R. is discussed in Dreyfus, *Vie politique*, p. 170; for the 1934 scheme, see *J. O. C. Débs.*, June 1, 1934, p. 1340.

58. "Mémoire sur la décentralisation de l'Alsace, de l'intendant militaire royaliste Coutillard," n.d. [1935], pp. 1–65. Arch.

H-R., Coll. Heitz, no cote number. A companion report—
"Mémoire royaliste sur la situation politique de l'Alsace au
début de 1934"—(probably the work of Fernand-Joseph
Heitz) is especially penetrating in its analysis of the U.P.R.;
see ibid., cote 2J 213 60, pp. 1–42.

59. Comte Jean de Pange, *Journal*, vol. 1, *1927–1930* (Paris,
1964), p. 139.

60. The quotation concerning the Action Française is taken from
Geneviève Baas, *Le malaise alsacien, 1919–1924* (Strasbourg,
1972), p. 139; for the fate of the Fédération Nationale Catho-
lique, see Adrien Dansette, *Religious History of Modern
France*, vol. 2, *Under the Third Republic*, trans. John Dingle
(New York, 1961), p. 349.

61. La Chambre was secretary of state for Alsace-Lorraine in
the cabinet of Premier Edouard Daladier at the time.

62. Dreyfus, *Vie politique*, pp. 216, 218–21, 245–48, 252; certain
U.P.R. members, however, did support the autonomists
Hueber and Heil (who ran for the seats from Strasbourg-
Sud and Soultz, respectively).

63. The other Alsatian members were Michel Walter, Thomas
Seltz, Henri Meck, Charles Elsässer, Edouard Fuchs, Joseph
Gullung, and Charles Hartmann.

64. Fernand L'Huillier, "L'Alsace contemporaine: un destin
exceptionnel," in Dollinger, *Histoire*, p. 477, 478; Jean-Marie
Mayeur, "Une bataille scolaire: les catholiques alsaciens et
la politique scolaire du gouvernement du Front Populaire,"
Cahiers de l'Association Interuniversitaire de l'Est (1962),
pp. 85–101.

65. Bickler, Mourer, and Hueber were arrested as were Rossé,
Stürmel, René Hauss, Victor Antoni, Paul Schall, Peter
Bieber (Bickler's law partner), Rudolf Lang (Bickler's
brother-in-law), René Schlegel, Abbé Joseph Brauner (di-
rector of the Strasbourg Municipal Archives), Dr. Joseph
Lefftz (chief of the Strasbourg Municipal Library), Jean
Keppi (erstwhile secretary of the Heimatbund), and Camille
Meyer (editor of the *Elsass-Lothringer Zeitung*).

CHAPTER 3

1. Justice, M-et-M., Dossier Rossé, liasse no. VIII, procès-verbal de l'audition de Wagner, Robert, le 15 décembre, 1945, cote C-29, p. 2; ibid., liasse no. VII, procès-verbal de l'audition de Bongartz, Albert, le 15 novembre, 1945, cote C-1, p. 2.

2. *Elsässer*, August 10, 1926, p. 1; Justice, M-et-M., Dossier de Nancy, liasse no. I (Information jusqu'en juin, 1940), procès-verbal d'interrogatoire ou de confrontation du nommé Rossé, le 23 novembre, 1939, cote C-21, pp. 2–3.

3. Dreyfus, *Vie politique*, pp. 209–10, 252; besides the *Elsässer Kurier*, the other dailies in Rossé's publishing empire were the *Mulhäuser Volksblatt*, *Guebwiller Volksblatt*, *Thanner Volksblatt*, *Schlettstadter Volksblatt*, and *Le Populaire du Sundgau*.

4. Charles Haenggi, "Mémoires. Drittes Buch: Kampfjahre im Elsass, 1926–1939" (manuscript, confidential source, Colmar, n.d. [1950]), pp. 516–76.

5. Arch. B-R., No. AL 98, paquet 674, vol. HI-79, Note sur les "Jeunesses de l'U.P.R.," et leurs relations avec les "Jungmännern" du Landespartei, le 12 juin, 1934, pp. 1–5; penciled note signed by Teichmann, personal assistant to Robert Ernst, the Gauleiter's adjutant, in Déf. nat., Procès Ernst, liasse no. 1, transmis téléphoniquement au Oberleutnant Rüdiger, le 12 juillet, 1940, cote 418.

6. Justice, M-et-M., Dossier de Nancy, liasse no. I, procès-verbal de l'audition de Becker, Antoine, Commissaire de police spéciale, le 6 janvier, 1940, cote C-55, pp. 2–6.

7. Arch. B-R., No. AL 98, paquet 674, vol. HI-79 (U.P.R., années 1933–1934), le Commissariat spécial de Mulhouse, Rapport, le 27 mars, 1934; ibid., le Contrôleur général à M. le Directeur général de la Sûreté nationale, no. 141, le 17 janvier, 1934, p. 1; see also note 55, Chapter 2.

8. For the effect of Alsatian attendance at the 1929 congress on the relations between the U.P.R. and Mgr. Ruch, bishop of Strasbourg, see Dreyfus, *Vie politique*, pp. 154–55.

9. Justice, M-et-M., Dossier de Nancy, liasse no. 1, lettre du Me. Treuer à M. le Colonel Laroubine, Juge d'instruction

près le Tribunal militaire de la 20e. région à Nancy, le 9 janvier, 1940, cote C-57.

10. Bongartz to Ernst, October 1, 1927, in Déf. nat., Procès Ernst, liasse no. 1, procès-verbal de l'interrogatoire du nommé Bongartz, Albert, le 10 septembre, 1946, cote 96, pp. 1–2; Bongartz to Ernst, August 25, 1927, ibid., Rapport d'ensemble des pièces 87 à 94 adressé par le Commissaire divisionnaire des renseignements généraux à Strasbourg à M. le Commissaire du Gouvernement près la Cour de justice du Haut-Rhin, cote 97, p. 3; ibid., liasse no. 2 (Instruction, deuxième partie), procès-verbal d'information du nommé Bongartz, Albert, le 11 juillet, 1947, cote 466, p. 4. Further information on the Rossé-Bongartz-Ernst connection is found in Justice, M-et-M., Dossier de Nancy, liasse no. I, le Contrôleur général de la Sûreté nationale à M. le capitaine Picard, Juge d'instruction près le Tribunal militaire permanent à Nancy, le 6 juin, 1940, cote C-89, p. 2.

11. Bongartz mentions Emile Pinck and Reverend Schreiber, deputy to the Reichstag during the Weimar period and professor of the Catholic faculty at the University of Münster. See Déf. nat., Procès Ernst, liasse no. 1, procès-verbal d'interrogatoire du nommé Bongartz, Albert, le 9 juillet, 1945, cote 196, pp. 12–13, 15.

12. Justice, M-et-M., Dossier de Nancy, liasse no. I, procès-verbal d'interrogatoire du nommé Mohrlock, Jean-Lucien, le 18 mars, 1940, cote C-76, pp. 2–4.

13. Déf. nat., Procès Ernst, liasse no. 1, déposition du témoin Mourer, Jean-Pierre, le 25 avril, 1947, cote 177, pp. 7–8; ibid., audition de l'Abbé Brauner, Joseph, le 28 février, 1939, cote 171, pp. 1–17.

14. Justice, M-et-M., Dossier de Nancy, liasse no. II (Information reprise en juin, 1945 devant le Tribunal militaire de Nancy puis devant la Cour de justice de Meurthe-et-Moselle), procès-verbal d'interrogatoire ou de confrontation du nommé Rossé, Joseph, le 25 juillet, 1945, cote C-95, pp. 1–10.

15. Germany, Bundesarchiv (Coblenz), R. 83, Elsass: Zentral Stellen der allgemeine Zivilverwaltung im 2, Weltkrieg im Elsass (Der Reichsstatthalter in Baden und Chef der Zivilverwaltung im Elsass), Nr. 72, Ermittlung der elsässischen

Volkstumkämpfer und deren Unterstützung nach ihrer Befreiung aus französischen Haft: 1940–1944 [hereafter cited as Bundesarchiv, R. 83], Deutsche Botschaft A2/9g, An das Auswärtiges Amt, 23 Juli, 1940, unnumbered cote.

16. France, Ministère d'Etat chargé de la Défense nationale, Direction de la Gendarmerie et de la Justice militaire . . . Dépôt central d'archives, Caserne Noëfort (Meaux), Tribunal militaire permanent de la 10e. région militaire séant à Strasbourg, Inventaire des pièces de la procédure suivie contre le nommé Wagner, Robert, sujet allemand, ex-Gauleiter d'Alsace . . . [hereafter cited as Déf. nat., Procès Wagner], procès-verbal d'interrogatoire ou de confrontation du nommé Wagner, Robert, le 7 février, 1946, liasse no. 1 (numéro de classement d'archive, 1), no cote number.

17. Déf. nat., Procès Ernst, liasse no. 1, Rapport établi par J-J. Marco, le 17 novembre, 1939, de la Maison d'arrêt (Nancy), cote 180, pp. 1–8; ibid., procès-verbal d'interrogatoire ou de confrontation du nommé Ernst, Robert, le 23 avril, 1947, cote 128, pp. 1–4; see also a frank account by Mourer in ibid., procès-verbal de l'audition de Mourer, J-P., le 29 mars, 1947, cote 126, pp. 1–4.

18. Arch. B-R., no. AL 98, paquet 672, vol. HI-66 (Jungmannschaft 1938–1939), le Contrôleur général de la Sûreté nationale à M. le Colonel Laroubine, Juge d'instruction près le Tribunal militaire permanent à Nancy, le 9 mars, 1940, unnumbered cote, pp. 1–3.

19. Déf. nat., Procès Ernst, liasse no. 2 (Instruction, 2e. partie), procès-verbal de la déposition du témoin Rossé, Joseph, le 20 mai, 1947, cote 429, pp. 1–7; Rossé's "denunciation" is in a letter to Camille Chautemps, secretary of state for Alsace-Lorraine, and is found in Justice, M-et-M., Dossier de Nancy, liasse no. I, lettre du Me. Treuer à M. le Colonel Laroubine, Juge d'instruction près le Tribunal militaire de la 20e. région à Nancy, le 3 février, 1940, cote C-67, p. 2.

20. Justice, M-et-M., Dossier de Nancy, liasse no. I, procès-verbal d'interrogatoire ou de confrontation du nommé Rossé, Joseph, le 23 novembre, 1939, cote C-21, pp. 2–3; ibid., Dossier Rossé, liasse no. VII (témoins), procès-verbal de l'audition de M. Felsenstein, Maxime, le 4 janvier, 1946, cote C-43, p. 2.

21. Justice, Procès Stürmel, dossier no. 1, IV (pièces parvenues à la Cour après la clôture de l'instruction), pièce 10, lettre de Jean Stürmel à M. le Commissaire du Gouvernement, le 4 janvier, 1947.

22. Arch. H-R., Procès des autonomistes, cote 35793, sous-cote 14, Stürmel, Marcel . . . procès-verbal de l'inculpé . . . le 20 mars, 1928, pp. 1–4.

23. Justice, Procès Stürmel, dossier no. 2, III (Scellés), no. 2, Direction générale de la Sûreté nationale, scellé no. 4, déposition du témoin Riehl, Henri, le 3 février, 1928, cote 5; . . . le 4 février, 1928, cotes 11a, 11b.

24. Procès Colmar (May 24, 1928), p. 234.

25. See Stürmel's open letter to Premier André Tardieu, October 30, 1930, in Arch. B-R., no. AL 98, paquet 686, vol. HI-117 (amnistiés Alsace-Lorraine), unnumbered cote.

26. Justice, Procès Stürmel, dossier no. 1, III (pièces d'information), extrait des déclarations de Bilger, Joseph, à la Sécurité militaire concernant Stürmel, le 19 juin, 1946, cote 284. For further information on Bilger, see note 57, this chapter.

27. See, for example, his vigorous intervention in the debate over the educational features of the 1934 Alsace-Lorraine budget (along with Rossé, Dahlet, Médard Brogly, Thomas Seltz, and Maurice Burrus), in J. O. C. Débs., January 25, 1934, pp. 332–35; January 26, 1934, pp. 362–63.

28. For the 1937–38 trial, see a vita sent by Stürmel to Ernst (the Gauleiter's assistant) to speed his entrance into the Nazi party in 1940: Justice, Procès Stürmel, dossier no. 2, III, scellé no. 1, pièce 1, M. Stürmel, bisherige Abgeordneter und Generalrat, an den Herrn Robert Ernst, Generalreferent beim Chef der Zivilverwaltung, le 6 novembre, 1940.

29. The root of the word is "Dumm," and it is found in several variations throughout Alsace: Dürmel in Strasbourg, Dermel in Sélestat, Dürmel in Mulhouse and the Sundgau; for the defamatory jingle, see Justice, Procès Stürmel, dossier no. 1, III, procès-verbal de l'audition du sieur Chapuis, Joseph, le 29 août, 1946, cote 358.

30. "Lebenslauf" (original typescript and signature), submitted by Stürmel to the Waffen SS recruiting bureau in Strasbourg, October 1, 1940, in ibid., dossier no. 1, III, no. 2, cotes 403–8.

31. Ibid., dossier no. 1, IV, lettre jointe avec la photocopie du rapport Léonard, cotes 53–54.

32. The bulk of the evidence concerning Stürmel and Scherer is found in ibid., dossier no. 1, III, no. 2 (pièces d'information), procès-verbal de l'audition de l'Abbé Brauner, Joseph, le 28 février, 1939, cotes 6–9, 15.

33. Ibid., le 4 mars, 1939, cote 26; Arch. H-R., Procès des autonomistes, cote 35793, Le Commissaire Chef de la Sûreté Boltz à M. le Juge d'instruction Mitton, le 12 mars, 1928, unnumbered cote, pp. 1–2.

34. Haenggi, "Mémoires," p. 592.

35. Interview, Marcel Stürmel, 28 July 1971, Altkirch (Haut-Rhin); "Lebenslauf," Justice, Procès Stürmel, dossier no. 1, III, no. 2, cote 405. For Stürmel's pecuniary rewards during the occupation, see Chapter 4.

36. Justice, Procès Mourer, II (Bulletin no. 2 et renseignements), cote 2.

37. Ibid., III (pièces d'information), chemise no. 1 (Interrogatoire sur charges), le 7 janvier, 1947, cote 18, p. 5.

38. Ibid.

39. Ibid., chemise no. 1, Interrogatoire du nommé Mourer, J-P., le 15 octobre, 1946, cote 17, pp. 1–5.

40. Ibid., Interrogatoire sur charges, le 7 janvier, 1947, cote 18, p. 5; ibid., chemise no. 4 (Activité de Mourer comme Kreisleiter), Stammbuch für Murer, Hans-Peter, den 10 März, 1941, IV, cote 4, p. 1.

41. Ibid., chemise no. 3 (Activité de Mourer avant 1940), III, cote 1, M. le Contrôleur général de la Sûreté nationale (Monnard) à M. le Directeur général de la Sûreté nationale, le 6 février, 1939, sous-cote 1, p. 11.

42. Ibid., chemise no. 1, Interrogatoire de Mourer, J-P., le 10 septembre, 1946, cote 12, p. 13.

43. Déf. nat., Procès Ernst, liasse no. 1, Rapport établi par J-J. Marco, le 17 octobre, 1939, de la Maison d'arrêt (Nancy), cote 180, pp. 1–8.

44. Justice, Procès Mourer, III, chemise no. 1, Interrogatoire sur charges, le 7 janvier, 1947, cote 18, pp. 6–7.

45. Ibid., pp. 22–24.

46. Ibid., p. 14. The descriptions of Hauss and Schall are by

Roos and are found in Déf. nat., Procès Ernst, liasse no. 1, Interrogatoire du nommé Bongartz, Albert, no date, cote 196, p. 9; that of Bickler is by Hauss and is found in the Marco report, in ibid., Rapport établi par J-J. Marco, le 17 octobre, 1939, de la Maison d'arrêt (Nancy), cote 180, p. 4.

47. Justice, Procès Mourer, III, chemise no. 2 (Rapports et pièces concernant le mouvement autonomiste), II, le Contrôleur général de la Sûreté nationale (Monnard) à M. le Directeur de la Sûreté nationale, le 28 avril, 1938, cote 5, pp. 30, 38–39; E. L. Z., July 29, 1939, p. 1.

48. Justice, Procès Mourer, III, chemise no. 3, déposition du témoin Knabbe, Erich, Affaire Mourer, le 4 octobre, 1946, cote 33, p. 3; ibid., chemise no. 1, Interrogatoire sur charges le 7 janvier, 1947, cote 18, p. 24; ibid., chemise no. 3, Confrontation entre Knabbe et Gehrum, Julius, le 4 octobre, 1946, cote 32, pp. 1–2; and testimony of Marc Kleindienst (natural son of Roos's second wife), in ibid., procès-verbal de la declaration du nommé Kleindienst, Marc, le 20 juillet, 1946, cote 23, pp. 1–2.

49. Ernst to Robert Wagner, Gauleiter of Baden-Elsass, May 9, 1942, in Déf. nat., Procès Ernst, liasse no. 1, cotes 235–36; audition du Dr. Robert Ernst contre Rossé, Joseph, le 12 mai, 1947, cote 240, pp. 3–4 (copy).

50. Bundesarchiv, R. 83, Nr. 34, Einsetzung den Kreisleiter der NSDAP im Elsass und Aufstellung der Schaltsfestsetzung, 1940–1942, Elsässischer Hilfsdienst Landestelle, an den Herrn Reichsstatthalter und Gauleiter Robert Wagner, den 7 Dezember, 1940, no. 1798, p. 9; the edict making Bickler a French subject was not handed down by the Cantonal Tribunal of Rohrbach-les-Bitche (Moselle) until February 12, 1921.

51. France. Ministère de la Justice. Cour de justice, section du Bas-Rhin, Archives du Haut-Rhin (Colmar), cote des archives 32267, Procès de Bickler, Armand Christian . . . avocat, inculpé du chef d'intelligence avec l'ennemi [hereafter cited as Justice, Procès Bickler], liasse no. 3 (pièces d'information), chemise no. 1 (L'activité de Bickler avant septembre, 1939), le Contrôleur général à M. le Préfet du Bas-Rhin, no. 11000, le 7 juillet, 1939, secret, cote C-4, pp.

2–3; for the student fraternities, see Arch. B-R., no. AL 98, paquet 686, vol. HI-114, folders 5, 8; for Bickler's activity in them and in the Heimatbund, see Justice, Procès Bickler, liasse no. 3, chemise no. 1, no. 11000, le 7 juillet, 1939, cote C-4, pp. 1–2. Another Protestant student fraternity, the Foyer chrétien de jeunes gens, was responsible for a hilarious report submitted to the French police which gives some idea of student sport at the university during the interwar years. The members of this group gave vent to a *"tapage [nocturne] dépassant toute mesure,"* with the "stupefying cacaphony" of German drinking songs accompanied by the shoving about of heavy furniture which drove the peaceful neighbors to insomnia and "extreme nervosity." The tribunal ordered the group to cease merry-making after 10:00 P.M. and to pay the legal costs of the suit. See ibid., III, chemise no. 1, Au tribunal de 1ère instance, Chambre civile, Strasbourg, le 2 juin, 1937, cote C-71, pp. 1–3.

52. Justice, Procès Bickler, liasse no. 3, chemise no. 1, cote C-4, pp. 8–18.

53. *Jungmannschaft* (Bibliothèque municipale de Strasbourg), February 21, 1931, p. 1.

54. Hermann Bickler, *Widerstand: Zehn Jahre Volkstumkampf der Elsass-Lothingrische Jungmannschaft* (Strasbourg, 1943), pp. 84–86; the contemporary effects of this affair and the connections with Ernst are analyzed in Dreyfus, *Vie politique,* pp. 174–75.

55. Justice, Procès Bickler, liasse no. 3, chemise no. 1, cote C-33, pp. 44–54, 82–83, 115–20.

56. Ibid., chemise no. 1, procés-verbal d'information du nommé Eyer, Frédéric-Charles, le 29 novembre, 1939, cote C-38, p. 5 (Eyer was also editor of *Frei Volk*); Bickler's denials are in ibid., Tribunal militaire permanent de la 20e. région militaire séant à Nancy, procès-verbal d'interrogatoire ou de confrontation de Bickler, Hermann, le 27 février, 1940, cote C-49, p. 6.

57. Dreyfus, *Vie politique,* p. 231; Arch. B-R., no. AL 98, paquet 672, vol. HI-65 (Bauernbund, 1935–1939), Le Contrôleur général de la Sûreté nationale à M. le Préfet de la Moselle, le 26 avril, 1938, unnumbered cote, pp. 1–4; paquet 694, vol.

HI-159, Police d'Etat de Strasbourg, Cabinet du Commissaire central, le 3 juillet, 1935, cote 14.

58. Justice, Procès Bickler, liasse no. 3, chemise no. 1, cote C-4, pp. 10, 13, 23–24.

59. Ibid., chemise no. 1, procès-verbal de l'audition de M. Eyer, Frédéric-Charles, devant le Commissaire de police spéciale, M. Becker, Antoine, le 1 octobre, 1938, cote C-20, pp. 1–2; *Frei Volk* ceased publication in May 1939.

60. Ibid., chemise no. 1, cote C-20, p. 18; for pre-Munich material, see Déf. nat., Procès Ernst, liasse no. 1, Le Contrôleur général de la Sûreté nationale (Monnard) à M. le Directeur général de la Sûreté nationale, le 28 avril, 1938, cote 12, pp. 13–14.

61. Justice, Procés Bickler, liasse no. 3, chemise no. 1, Le Contrôleur général du surveillance du territoire, circonscription de Strasbourg, à M. le Préfet du Bas-Rhin, le 15 octobre, 1938, cote 3, 8; Procès Stürmel, dossier no. 1, III, no. 2, cote 107, p. 1. See also, Arch. B-R., no. AL 98, paquet 670, vol. HI-63 (L'autonomisme breton et les autonomistes alsaciens), le Commissaire divisionnaire à M. le Directeur général de la Sûreté nationale, le 15 octobre, 1934, unnumbered cote, pp. 1–2.

62. Justice, Procès Bickler, liasse no. 3, chemise no. 1, procès-verbal d'information du nommé Marco, Julien, le 12 octobre, 1939, cote C-59, pp. 1–3.

63. Ibid., Tribunal militaire permanent de la 20e. région militaire séant à Nancy, procès-verbal d'information du nommé Kaufmann, Jean Albert, le 20 mars, 1940, cote C-51, p. 3; Déf. nat., Procès Ernst, liasse no. 1, Rapport établi par J-J. Marco, le 17 octobre, 1939, de la Maison d'arrèt (Nancy), cote 180, pp. 1–8. Bickler's denials of these developments are in Justice, Procès Bickler, liasse no. 3, chemise no. 1, procès-verbal d'interrogatoire ou de confrontation du nommé Bickler, Hermann, le 27 février, 1940, cote C-49, pp. 6–7.

64. Justice, Procès Bickler, liasse no. 3, chemise no. 1, Le Commissaire divisionnaire de police spécial à M. le Colonel Laroubine, Juge d'instruction militaire près le Tribunal militaire de Nancy, le 18 avril, 1940 [perquisition opérée

à l'étude de Mes. Bieber et Bickler, le 28 mars, 1940], cote C-55, pp. 2–5, 9.

65. For Bickler's contacts with the Toepfer brothers, see ibid., chemise no. 1, Tribunal militaire permanent de la 20e. région militaire séant à Nancy, procès-verbal d'interrogatoire ou de confrontation du nommé Bickler, Hermann, le 27 février, 1940, cote C-49, pp. 3–4.

66. See the very forthright and frank evidence given by Mourer, under sentence of death, in ibid., chemise no. 2 (Réquisitoire, mandat d'arrêt, procès-verbaux, interrogatoires de l'Affaire Bickler, cotes 1–35), procès-verbal d'interrogatoire du nommé Mourer, Jean-Pierre, le 29 mars 1947, cote 35, pp. 1–3.

67. Ibid., chemise no. 1, Le Directeur général de la Sûreté nationale, le 9 septembre, 1939, cote C-12, p. 1.

68. Ibid., chemise no. 1, lettre à M. le Juge d'instruction, de Bickler, Armand, le 26 avril, 1940, cote C-56; procès-verbal d'interrogatoire du nommé Marco, Julien, le 27 avril, 1940, cote C-59, p. 3.

69. The anti-French attitude of Spieser's ancestors is described by him in France, Ministère de la Justice, Cour de justice, section du Bas-Rhin . . . Archives du Haut-Rhin (Colmar), cote des archives 32298, Procès de Spieser, Frédéric . . . château de la Hunabourg, inculpé d'intelligence avec l'ennemi [hereafter cited as Justice, Procès Spieser], III (Pièces d'information), chemise no. 3, III, Service régional des renseignements généraux, Strasbourg, au sujet de Ernst, Robert, pièce 18 ("Observations préliminaires," 1933–1934); the characterization of Spieser's father is found in ibid., II (Renseignements), Le Tribunal militaire permanent de la 20e région militaire séant à Nancy . . . , unnumbered cote.

70. Ibid., III, chemise no. 3, III, pièce 18; Déf. nat., Procès Ernst, liasse no. 1, Le Contrôleur général de la Sûreté nationale (Monnard) à M. le Directeur général de la Sûreté nationale, le 28 avril, 1939, cote 12, p. 28.

71. Justice, Procès Spieser, III, chemise no. 3, III, pièce 18; Déf. nat., Procès Ernst, liasse no. 1, Le Contrôleur général de la Sûreté nationale (Monnard) à M. le Directeur général de la Sûreté nationale, le 28 avril, 1939, cote 12, p. 29.

72. Déf. nat., Procès Ernst, liasse no. 1, Le Contrôleur général de la Sûreté nationale (Monnard) à M. le Directeur général de la Sûreté nationale, le 28 avril, 1939, cote 12, p. 29.
73. Justice, Procès Spieser, III, chemise no. 3, III, pièce 18; Toepfer to Ernst, January 27, 1932 (emphasizes that the name of the donor and his connection with the project must be kept secret), ibid., pièces 1–1a.
74. Ibid., piecès 2–2a.
75. Ernst to Toepfer, September 17, 1932 (which states that the former will "mobilize what is necessary on my side"), ibid., pièce 4.
76. Toepfer to Ernst, September 20, 1932, ibid., pièce 5.
77. Undated memorandum by Spieser entitled "Financial arrangements (a proposition)," ibid., pièce 25. The Verein für das Deutschum im Ausland money was an interest-free loan guaranteed by Spieser's brother-in-law, Prince Alexander zu Dohna-Schlobitten.
78. Déf. nat., Procès Ernst, liasse no. 1, Le Contrôleur général de la Sûreté nationale (Monnard) à M. le Directeur général de la Sûreté nationale, le 28 avril, 1938, cote 12, p. 30. The correspondence between Spieser and Ernst is found in Justice, Procès Spieser, III, chemise no. 3, III, pièce 9.
79. Justice, Procès Spieser, III, chemise no. 3, III, pièce 14.
80. Tausend Brücken: Eine biographische Erzählung aus dem Schicksal eines Landes (Stuttgart; 1952).
81. Spieser to Ernst, April 5, 1935, in Justice, Procès Spieser, III, chemise no. 3, III, pièce 9.
82. Ibid., pièce 16, undated document.
83. "Ziele" and "Song-weeks, folk dances, and theater," ibid., pièces 19, 21.
84. Interview, Madame Marguerite Hauth-Boeckel, July 29, 1972. Secrecy about the Hünenburg's real purpose as far as the architects and even the venerable Abbé Louis Pinck were concerned is emphasized in Justice, Procès Spieser, III, chemise no. 3, III, pièce 22. (Paul Schmitthenner, an Alsatian architect very famous for his work in Germany was originally selected to build the Hünenburg but due to his heavy work schedule, the assignment was given to one of his pupils, Karl Loebel, who was half-Jewish; Loebel was

hidden by the Boeckel family of Mittelbergheim, Bas-Rhin, at their Hohwald chalet during the German occupation of Alsace.)

85. Justice, Procès Spieser, III, chemise no. 3, III, pièce 18.
86. Ibid., pièce 24; see also pièce 22.
87. Justice, Procès Stürmel, dossier no. 1, III, no. 2, Le Contrôleur général de surveillance du territoire, circonscription régionale de Strasbourg, le 28 avril, 1938, cote 92.
88. Arch. B-R., no. AL 98, paquet 694, vol. HI-159, Le Préfecture du Bas-Rhin . . . à M. le Président du Conseil, le 8 juin, 1937, le 7 mars, 1938, cotes 114, 174; Justice, Procès Spieser, III, chemise no. 1 (L'activité de Spieser avant et pendant la guerre), cotes 3, 9, 12.
89. Ibid., III, chemise no. 1, cotes 3, 9, 12.
90. Spieser's vita in the *Strassburger Neueste Nachrichten*, July 28, 1941, p. 1.
91. Spieser to Hitler, September 10, 1939, in Justice, Procès Spieser, III, chemise no. 1, cote 36, pp. 1–8.
92. The 1938 agreement between France and Germany to "recognize solemnly as definitive the frontier between the two countries as presently traced" is found in T-120/912/383202 (Deutsch-französische Abkommen vom 6.12.38); Justice, Procès Spieser, III, chemise no. 1, Der Staatsminister und Chef der Präsidialkanzlei des Führers und Reichskanzlers, den 21 September, 1939, cotes 34–35.
93. Interview between Spieser, Dr. Hohlfeld, and Dr. Peter, July 15, 1937, in Justice, Procès Spieser, III, chemise no. 1, cote 9, p. 1.
94. Déf. nat., Procès Ernst, liasse no. 1, procès-verbal d'interrogatoire ou de confrontation du nommé Ernst, Robert, le 7 mai, 1947, cote 183, pp. 1–4; Ernst, *Rechenschaftsbericht eines Elsässers* (Berlin, 1954), p. 215.
95. Déf. nat., Procès Ernst, liasse no. 1, procès-verbal d'interrogatoire ou de confrontation, le 2 février, 1947, cote 30, p. 4.
96. Ibid., pièces annexes dans la procédure contre le docteur Robert Ernst, liasse no. 1 (Inventaire), cote C-9, sous-cotes 1–13.
97. Ibid., Bericht über (1.) Deutscher Schutzbund, (2.) Volksdeutscher Klub e. V., (3.) Schutzvereinhaus GmbH, Berlin,

den 13 Dezember, 1937, cote C-6, pp. 1–70; liasse no. 1, procès-verbal d'interrogatoire ou de confrontation du nommé Ernst, Robert, le 4 juillet, 1946, cote 15, p. 4.

98. Ibid., liasse no. 1, procès-verbal d'interrogatoire ou de confrontation du nommé Ernst, Robert, le 7 mai, 1947, cote 183, p. 4; cf. ibid., liasse no. 1, procès-verbal de la déposition du témoin Rossé, Joseph, le 20 mai, 1947, cote 429, pp. 1–7.

99. For Ernst's role in the Steinacher affair, see Hans-Adolf Jacobsen, ed., *Hans Steinacher, Bundesleiter des V.D.A. 1933–1937: Errinerungen und Dokumente* (Boppard-am-Rhein, 1970), pp. xxvii–xxviii, 309–10 (letter, Ernst to Steinacher, June 20, 1935); Déf. nat., Procès Ernst, liasse no. 2 (Instruction 2e. partie), procès-verbal d'interrogatoire ou de confrontation du nommé Ernst, Robert, le 19 août, 1947, cote 495, pp. 1–5.

100. Déf. nat., Procès Ernst, liasse no. 2, procès-verbal d'interrogatoire ou de confrontation du nommé Ernst, Robert, le 19 août, 1947, cote 495, p. 6.

101. Ibid., Extrait du procès Wagner . . . déposition du Dr. Robert Ernst, le 29 avril, 1946, cote 431, p. 2.

CHAPTER 4

1. Justice, Procès Mourer, III, chemise no. 11 (pièces arrivées après la clôture de l'information), Der Kreisleiter des Kreis Mühlhausen im Elsass an Herrn Major Dr. Ernst, Generalreferent beim Chef der Zivilverwaltung, den 23 Juli, 1941, cote 50.

2. *Aux écoutes*, April 21, 1940, p. 1; for the angry reply of Rossé's lawyers that the author of the article had seen the secret Nancy dossiers, see Justice, M-et-M., Dossier de Nancy, liasse no. I, cotes C-84 and C-86; for Stürmel, see Justice, Procès Stürmel, procès-verbal de l'audition de l'abbé Brauner, Joseph, le 28 février, 1940, cotes 6–9, 15, 26; for Bickler, see Justice, Procès Bickler, procès-verbal d'information du nommé Kaufmann, Jean Albert, le 20 mars, 1940, cote C-51, p. 3.

3. Déf. nat., Procès Ernst, procès-verbal de l'audition de Mourer, Jean-Pierre, le 1 avril, 1947, cote 121, p. 5; Justice,

Procès Mourer, III, chemise no. 1, Interrogatoire sur charges du nommé Mourer, Jean-Pierre, le 7 janvier, 1947, cote C-18, pp. 31–39; chemise 4 (Activité de Mourer comme Kreisleiter), déposition du témoin Ernst, Robert (confrontation avec Mourer, J-P.), le 11 décembre, 1946, cote C-66, pp. 1–12.

4. Déf. nat., Procès Ernst, liasse no. 1, déposition du témoin Ernst, Robert, le 11 décembre, 1946, cote 103, pp. 4–5; procès-verbal de l'audition de Mourer, J-P., le 1 avril, 1947, cote 121, p. 5. On Wagner, see note 6, this chapter, and Peter Hüttenberger, *Die Gauleiter: Studie zum Wandel des Machtgefüges in der NSDAP* (Stuttgart, 1969), p. 14.

5. Photocopy of original manuscript in Ernst's handwriting in Def. nat., Procès Ernst, liasse no. 1, instruction, première partie, cote 267, pp. 1–2.

6. Norman Rich, *Hitler's War Aims*, vol. 2, *The Establishment of the New Order* (New York, 1974), p. 142; for the Freudenstadt conference, see Déf. nat., Procès Wagner, liasse no. 1, procès-verbal des déclarations de Lammers, Heinrich, le 11 avril, 1946, cote 102, pièce 7. In his definitive work on German policy toward France during the Second World War, Eberhard Jaeckel asserts that the Freudenstadt conference did not take place—that Hitler was in his Belgian headquarters at the time—but states that Wagner knew of his assignment before June 19, the date on which he was appointed to his new functions. (The unpublished decree confirming Wagner in his duties was issued on August 2, 1940.) See Jaeckel's *Frankreich in Hitlers Europa: Die deutsche Frankreichpolitik im zweiten Weltkrieg* (Stuttgart, 1966), pp. 76 n. 9, 79.

7. Déf. nat., Procès Ernst, liasse no. 3, procès-verbal d'interrogatoire ou de confrontation du nommé Ernst, Robert, le 5 février, 1954, cote 667, p. 3; liasse no. 1, procès-verbal d'interrogatoire ou de confrontation du nommé Ernst, le 28 mai, 1947, cote 274, p. 3.

8. Justice, M-et-M., Dossier Rossé, liasse no. IX (Interrogatoire récapitulatif), procès-verbal de l'inculpé Rossé, Joseph, le 27 mars, 1946, unnumbered cote, pp. 4–6.

9. Ernst's admissions are in Justice, Procès Stürmel, dossier no.

1, III (Pièces d'information), procès-verbal de la déposition du Dr. Robert Ernst, le 28 juin, 1946, cote 312; cf. his entirely different account (which has Ernst telling Wagner that autonomism was not a camouflage for reannexation by the Reich, but a struggle for survival within the French cadre) in his *Rechenschaftsbericht*, p. 261. The phrase "mise en quarantaine" is Mourer's and is found in Justice, Procès Mourer, III, chemise no. 1, Interrogatoire sur charges du nommé Mourer, J-P., le 7 janvier, 1947, cote C-18, p. 1.

10. Justice, M-et-M., Dossier Rossé, liasse no. VI (Interrogatoire), procès-verbal d'interrogatoire de l'inculpé nommé Rossé, Joseph, le 13 novembre, 1945, unnumbered cote, pp. 8–12.

11. Déf. nat., Procès Ernst, liasse no. 1, procès-verbal de l'audition de Mourer, J-P., le 1 avril, 1947, cote 121, p. 5; Justice, Procès Mourer, III, chemise no. 1, Interrogatoire sur charges du nommé Mourer, J-P., le 7 janvier, 1947, cote C-18, p. 36; for Bickler's and Bieber's attitude, see Justice, Procès Bickler, liasse no. 3, chemise no. 2 (Réquisitoire, mandat d'arrêt, procès-verbaux, interrogatoires de l'Affaire Bickler), interrogatoire du nommé Bieber, Pierre, le 19 février, 1947, cote 32, p. 3; for Meyer's claims that he did not belong to the separatist side, but actually drew up the substitute phrase (referred to below), see Déf. nat., Procès Ernst, liasse no. 1, procés-verbal d'information du nommé Meyer, Camille, le 9 avril, 1947, cote 191, p. 2.

12. Justice, Procès Stürmel, dossier no. 1, III, chemise no. 2, (pièces d'information), procès-verbal d'interrogatoire, le 13 février, 1946, cote 468.

13. Déf. nat., Procès Ernst, liasse no. 1, procès-verbal de la déposition du témoin Rossé, Joseph, le 20 avril, 1947; liasse no. 2 (Instruction, 2e. partie), cote 429, p. 5. Rossé's testimony is confirmed by Jean Keppi in ibid., liasse no. 3 (Instruction, 3e. partie), notes d'audience, Affaire Ernst, audition du 11 janvier, 1955, cote 738, p. 9.

14. Jaeckel, *Frankreich*, p. 84.

15. *Siebenbürgisch-Deutsches Tagblatt*, June 25, 1940, p. 1; Germany, Bundesarchiv (Coblenz), R. 57, Deutsches Ausland-Institut, Stuttgart [hereafter cited as Bundesarchiv, R.

57], DAI 817, box no. 17 (Elsass 5–9), no. 40/3565. Those who spoke only dialect numbered 108,000; dialect and German, 503,000; dialect and French, 119,000.

16. Professor X., "Journal de guerre, 1940–1945" (typescript, confidential source, Colmar), January 3, 1941, p. 141; hopes for autonomy and confidence that the Germans would treat the Alsatians well are recorded in entries for June 14 and July 28, 1940 (pp. 5, 27).

17. Germany, Bundesarchiv (Coblenz), R. 58, Reichssicherheitshauptamt, Der Reichsführer-SS und Chef der deutschen Polizei, Der Chef der Sicherheitspolizei und des S. D. Amt III, Meldungen aus dem Reich, Geheim! [hereafter cited as Bundesarchiv, R. 58, Meldungen], Nr. 100, den 27 Juni, 1940, pp. 12–14.

18. Bundesarchiv, R. 57, DAI 165, pp. 18–19 (fol. 548–49), Dr. Czaki, Leiter vom Deutsches Ausland-Institut, Volkspolitische Grenzfahrt durch die deutsch-besiedelten Teile der besetzten Gebiete im Westen, den 12 Juli, 1940.

19. 300,000 Alsatians were repatriated by mid-October, 1940; see *Strassburger Neueste Nachrichten*, October 18, 1940, p. 1. The original French evacuation plans are found in Arch. B-R., no. AL 98, paquet 281, vol. B-IV-12–14. An anti-French song, "La chanson des réfugiés de 1939," brought by a soldier on leave from the front to Périgueux is also found in paquet 281, vol. HI-2, Le Contrôleur général de la Sûreté nationale à Limoges à M. le Directeur général de la Sûreté nationale à Paris, le 29 décembre, 1939, unnumbered pièce, annexe 1.

20. For the Hitlerjugend, see Germany, *Verordnungsblatt des Chefs der Zivilverwaltung im Elsass*, 4 vols. (Strasbourg, 1940–44) [hereafter cited as *Verordnungsblatt*], August 16, 1940, 1:10–11; for the Reichsarbeitsdienst, 1941, 2:362; for the Nuremberg laws, 1941, 2:580–81; for the confiscation and sale of French property, 1941, 2:740; for the Germanization of names, 1943, 4:22. Total confiscations and damages are rated at 160,864,000RM in Déf. nat., Procès Wagner, liasse no. 2, scellé no. 10, procès-verbal d'interrogatoire ou de confrontation du nommé Wagner, Robert, le 5 mars, 1946, cote 29, p. 4; an entire file of ninety documents on the *béret*

basque question, running from September 14, 1940, to June 5, 1944, is found in Bundesarchiv (Coblenz), R. 83, Nr. 81, Verbot des Tragen, Herstellens und Verkauf von französischen Uniformstücken sowie von Baskenmützen und dergleichen, 1940–1944.

21. Bundesarchiv R. 58, Meldungen Nr. 108, den 25 Juli, 1940, pp. 11–13.

22. Ibid., Meldungen Nr. 122, den 9 September, 1940, pp. 12–13; Nr. 128, den 30 September, 1940, pp. 13–15; Nr. 133, den 17 Oktober, 1940, pp. 12–13; Nr. 160, den 6 Februar, 1941, pp. 8–9; Nr. 178, den 10 April, 1941, pp. 16–20; Nr. 200, den 7 Juli, 1941, pp. 15–17.

23. Bundesarchiv, R. 57, DAI 888, box no. 19 (Elsass-Lothringen II), no. 3981; Professor X., "Journal," July 31, 1940, p. 31; September 26, 1940, p. 72; June 26, 1941, p. 205.

24. Wagner later testified that Hitler decided to introduce conscription in Alsace on his (Wagner's) suggestion; Keitel confirmed that Wagner favored the measure but left the decision to the führer. See Déf. nat., Procès Wagner, liasse no. 3 (Notes d'audience), audience du 24 avril, 1946, cote 125, p. 6; liasse no. 1 (inventaire des pièces de la procédure . . .), procès-verbal des déclarations de Keitel, le 12 avril, 1946, cote 4. Earlier correspondence between Wagner, Bormann, and others regarding conscription is found in liasse no. 2 (Duplicata Wagner), scellés ouverts, no. 6.

25. Ibid., liasse no. 2, Mémoires présentés par Robert Wagner à M. le Juge d'instruction, le 10 mars, 1946, cote 49, rapport no. 1, p. 9; liasse no. 1, procès-verbal d'interrogatoire ou de confrontation, le 11 mars, 1946, cote 41, p. 8. At an undated interview with Hitler during the autumn of 1940, neither the führer nor Ribbentrop nor Lammers nor Stuckart mentioned to Wagner any violation of international law in the question of Alsace's incorporation into the Reich. See ibid., procès-verbal d'interrogatoire ou de confrontation, le 5 mars, 1946, cote 29, p. 2.

26. Déf. nat., Procès Ernst, liasse no. 3, procès-verbal d'interrogatoire ou de confrontation du nommé Ernst, Robert, le 5 février, 1954, cote 667, p. 3; the whole series of official

French protests against the reannexation of Alsace is contained in Déf nat., Procès Wagner, liasse no. 2, Les Allemands et l'Alsace-Lorraine, correspondance entre la Délégation française de l'armistice et la Commission allemande de l'armistice, août et décembre, 1943, cote 65.

27. Déf. nat., Procès Wagner, liasse no. 2, Mémoires présentés par Robert Wagner à M. le Juge d'instruction, le 10 mars, 1946, cote 49, rapport no. 3, p. 1.

28. The court case involved Marcel Weinum, eighteen years old, who was caught trying to cross the Swiss frontier with several comrades; Wagner, called as a witness, pleaded unsuccessfully with the judge not to sentence the young man to die. See Professor X., "Journal," April 11, 1941, p. 324.

29. Déf. nat., Procès Wagner, liasse no. 3, audience du 25 avril, 1946, unnumbered cote, p. 15.

30. Déf. nat., Procès Ernst, liasse no. 2, procès-verbal d'interrogatoire ou de confrontation du nommé Ernst, Robert, le 18 juillet, 1947, cote 493, pp. 5–7; Ernst's solicitude for his Gaullist relatives is mentioned in Professor X., "Journal," June 28, 1941, p. 213; Ernst's origins as a "Welschlinge der Oberschicht" are emphasized in Bundesarchiv, R. 57, DAI 817, box no. 19, no. 3981, Anlage zum Reisebericht vom 4 Juli, 1941, Beobachtung und Eindrücke aus dem Elsass, p. 4.

31. See an undated letter to Ernst from Alsatian parents reproaching him for having promised that Alsatians would never be mobilized, in Déf. nat., Procès Ernst, liasse no. 2, cote 457, pièce 25.

32. Ibid., procès-verbal d'interrogatoire ou de confrontation du nommé Ernst, Robert, le 17 juillet, 1947, cote 471, p. 6.

33. Déf. nat., Procès Wagner, liasse no. 2, Mémoires présentés par Robert Wagner à M. le Juge d'instruction, le 10 mars, 1946, cote 49, rapport no. 2, p. 5; liasse no. 2, scellés ouverts, nos. 5a, 5b, affaire dite de Ballersdorf. Wagner's confession of his role in the affair is in ibid., liasse no. 3, audience du 25 avril, 1946, p. 10; Ernst's objections are found in Déf. nat., Procès Ernst, liasse no. 1, procès-verbal de confrontation entre Ernst et Wagner, le 1 août, 1946, cote 26, p. 3.

34. See Christian Wilsdorf, "Les incidents provoquées à Kaysers-

berg et à Orbey par les conseils de révision, les 14 et 15 février, 1943," typescript, Archives du Haut-Rhin, Colmar [1960], pp. 1–16; Ernst, *Rechenschaftsbericht*, p. 362; *Kolmarer Kurier*, February 25, 1943, p. 2.

35. The figures are drawn from the account of Robert Bailliard (Président de l'Association des évadés et incorporés de de force, groupement du Bas-Rhin), "Historique du rapatriement des Alsaciens incorporés de force," *Saisons d'Alsace* 39–40 (summer-autumn 1971): 482. The memoirs of the chief of the French Repatriation Mission to the Soviet Union during 1945 and 1946 are also useful: see, General Pierre Keller, *Au temps de Staline: A la recherche des prisonniers libérés en U.R.S.S.* (Paris, 1960), pp. 105–31. Of the many *récits* of the "malgré nous," the most famous is Guy Sajer, *Le soldat oublié* (Paris, 1967); see also, Armand Zahner, *Le soldat honteux: J'etais un "malgré-nous"* (Mulhouse, 1972). The "tragic comedy" quotation is drawn from Lothar Kettenacker, *Nationalsozialistische Volkstumspolitik im Elsass* (Stuttgart, 1973), p. 270.

36. T-120/737/35723-4, Der Chef der Zivilverwaltung im Elsass an den Stellvertreter des Führers, Reichsleiter Martin Bormann, den 22 April, 1941, Nr. 2430. Wagner's attitude is summed up in Déf. nat., Procès Ernst, liasse no. 1, procès-verbal d'interrogatoire ou de confrontation du nommé Ernst, Robert, le 20 mai, 1947, cote 241, pp. 2–3.

37. The creation of the Hilfsdienst is described in Justice, Procès Spieser, III, chemise no. 3, unnumbered folder, pièce 25, Der Oberstadtkommissar Strassburg im Elsass . . . an den Herrn Paul Schall, den 19 April, 1941, p. 1; Ernst's description is found in Déf. nat., Procès Ernst, liasse no. 2, procès-verbal d'interrogatoire ou de confrontation du nommé Ernst, Robert, le 29 avril, 1947, cote 373, pp. 1–2; for the poster, see Justice, Procès Spieser, III, chemise no. 3, unnumbered folder, pièce 16.

38. Justice, Procès Stürmel, dossier no. 1, III, no. 2, cote 208 (*Mühlhauser Tagblatt*, August 13, 1940), pp. 4–5; see also, cotes 367–71 and dossier no. 2, I, chemise no. 2 (extraits de journaux, 1940–1941), cotes 1–17. Stürmel's defense is in ibid., dossier no. 1, III, no. 2, procès-verbal d'interrogatoire

du nommé Stürmel, Marcel, le 13 février, 1946, cote 468, p. 2. For Rossé, see Justice, M-et-M., Dossier Rossé, liasse no. VIII (Conférences), cotes 1–5; his defense is in ibid., liasse no. VI (Interrogatoires), procès-verbal d'interrogatoire d'inculpé, le 18 décembre, 1945, cote 5, pp. 3, 8.

39. Justice, M-et-M., Dossier Rossé, liasse no. VII (témoins), déposition du témoin Oberlechner, Louis, le 15 janvier, 1946, cote C-57, p. 3; procès-verbal de l'audition de Bongartz, Albert, le 7 janvier, 1946, cote C-45, p. 1. For Mourer's later speeches as Kreisleiter, see note 110, this chapter.

40. Justice, Procès Spieser, III, chemise no. 3, I, unnumbered folder, pièce 11 (*Strassburger Neuste Nachrichten*, December 2, 1940, p. 1).

41. See Bundesarchiv, R. 83, Nr. 72 (Ermittlung der elsässischen Volkstumkämpfer), no cote numbers.

42. Verordnung über die deutsche Staatsangehörigkeit im Elsass vom 24 August, 1942, *Verordnungsblatt*, 1942, 3:251–52.

43. Déf. nat., Procès Ernst, liasse no. 1, audition du Dr. R. Ernst . . . c/ Rossé, Joseph, le 13 février, 1947, unnumbered cote, pp. 6–7.

44. Justice, Procès Bickler, III, chemise no. 2 (Réquisitoire), information du 11 mai, 1946, du nommé Wagner, Robert, cote 15, pp. 1–2.

45. Wagner's description of Bickler is in ibid., procès-verbal d'audition de R. Wagner, le 27 février, 1946, cote 14, p. 6; of Mourer, in Justice, Procès Mourer, III, chemise no. 4, procès-verbal de l'audition de Wagner, R., le 12 avril, 1946, cote 4, C-9, p. 1.

46. Justice, Procès Stürmel, dossier no. 1, III, no. 2 (Pièces d'information), An den Befehlshaber der Staatspolizei und des S. D., SS-Oberführer Dr. Scheel, den 19 Oktober, 1940, cote 203; An den Chef der Zivilverwaltung, Personalamt, Strassburg, den 1 Februar, 1943, cote 198.

47. Justice, M-et-M., Dossier Rossé, liasse no. IV, cote C-19, p. 1; liasse no. VI (Interrogatoires), procès-verbal d'interrogatoire de l'inculpé nommé Rossé, Joseph, le 27 février, 1946, cote 101, pp. 6–11.

48. Ibid., liasse no. VI, Interrogatoire du nommé Keppi, Jean, le 7 février, 1946, cote C-88, p. 2; procès-verbal d'interroga-

toire de l'inculpé nommé Rossé, Joseph, le 18 janvier, 1946, cote 15, p. 4.

49. Ibid., liasse no. IV, scellé no. 1, An den Herrn General-referent beim Chef der Zivilverwaltung, Strassburg, den 7 November, 1940, cote 2. Rossé's party number was 7.848.492.

50. Ibid., J. Rossé an den Chef der Zivilverwaltung, Persönliche Abteilung, den 6 Juli, 1941, cote 2; ibid., liasse no. VII, pro-cès-verbal de l'audition de M. Brogly, Médard, le 11 janvier, 1946, unnumbered cote, pp. 3–4.

51. Ibid., liasse no. IV, Der Chef der Zivilverwaltung im Elsass, Verwaltungs- und Polizeiabteilung, den 29 Juli, 1943, cote 6. Rossé's justification of these payments is in liasse no. IV, procès-verbal d'interrogatoire d'inculpé nommé Rossé, Jo-seph, le 8 janvier, 1946, unnumbered cote, pp. 4–6.

52. Haenggi, "Mémoires," p. 620.

53. France, Ministère de la Justice, Archives départementales de Meurthe-et-Moselle (Nancy), Dossier contre Rossé, Joseph, Dossier Alsatia [hereafter cited as Justice, M-et-M., Dossier Alsatia], liasse no. IV, procès-verbal d'interrogatoire d'in-culpé Rossé, Joseph, le 20 février, 1946, cote 1, p. 18.

54. See Justice, M-et-M., Dossier Rossé, liasse no. IX, Interroga-toire récapitulatif du 11 mars, 1946, unnumbered cote, p. 56; for supporting evidence, see ibid., Dossier Alsatia, liasse no. III, audition de M. Brogly, Médard, le 10 janvier, 1946, cote C-24, pp. 1–2; concessions to the Germans are enumer-ated in ibid., Dossier Alsatia, liasse no. IV, procès-verbal d'inculpé nommé Rossé, Joseph, undated, cote C-23, p. 4.

55. Ibid., Dossier Rossé, liasse no. VII, procès-verbal de l'audition de Wagner, Robert, le 15 décembre, 1945, cote C-29, p. 2.

56. Ibid., liasse no. IX, interrogatoire récapitulatif du 11 mars, 1946, unnumbered cote, pp. 52–57.

57. Ibid., liasse no. VII, procès-verbal de la déposition du témoin Schuman, Robert, le 25 février, 1946, cote C-112, pp. 1–2.

58. The Rossé quotation is taken from ibid., liasse no. VI, procès-verbal d'interrogatoire ou de confrontation du nommé Rossé, Joseph, le 8 janvier, 1946, cote 11, pp. 8–12; the Wagner quotation is found in ibid., liasse no. VII, procès-verbal de

l'audition de Wagner, Robert, le 12 décembre, 1945, cote C-29, pp. 3–4.

59. On this point, see the testimony of Wagner in ibid., liasse no. VII, procès-verbal de l'audition du nommé Wagner, Robert, le 15 décembre, 1945, cote C-29, p. 2; see also the evidence presented by Rossé himself in a memoir entitled "Mon attitude et mon action en Alsace occupée par les Allemands de 1940 à 1945," ibid., Dossier Nancy, cote C-94, p. 8. Confirmation of Rossé's points is found in ibid., Dossier Rossé, liasse no. VII, procès-verbal de l'audition de M. Brogly, Médard, le 11 janvier, 1946, cote C-55, p. 2.

60. Ibid., Dossier Rossé, liasse no. VII, procès-verbal de l'audition de M. Fay, Bernard, le 20 décembre, 1945, cote C-38, pp. 1–3. Of the growing literature on the resistance in Alsace, the following are useful: Fernand l'Huillier, *Libération de l'Alsace* (Paris, 1975), pp. 36–59; Charles Bené, *L'Alsace dans les griffes nazies*, 3 vols. (Raon l'Etape, 1971–75), 1:103–282, 2:101–336, 3:189–364.

61. Justice, M-et-M., Dossier Rossé, liasse no. IX, procès-verbal d'interrogatoire d'inculpé nommé Rossé, Joseph, le 27 mars, 1946, unnumbered cote, pp. 10, 12.

62. Ibid., liasse no. VI, procès-verbal d'interrogatoire d'inculpé nommé Rossé, Joseph, le 8 janvier, 1946, cote 11, pp. 14–16; liasse no. VII, déposition du témoin Bas, André, le 21 janvier, 1946, cote C-65, p. 2.

63. Nazi suspicions of Rossé are confirmed in note 46, this chapter, and in Robert Heitz, "Rapport d'Alsace fait pour la France combattante, octobre, 1941"; see this resistant's *A mort (souvenirs)* (Paris, 1946), p. 288. The German report referred to is An die persönliche Abteilung Pg. Gaedeke, Strassburg, nr. 20 106/1, den 30 Juni, 1944, in Bundesarchiv, R. 83, Nr. 72.

64. Justice, M-et-M., Dossier Rossé, liasse no. IX, Interrogatoire récapitulatif, p. 65; liasse no. VII, procès-verbal de l'audition de M. Walter, Michel, le 25 janvier, 1946, cote C-69, p. 1; déposition du témoin Bas, André, le 21 janvier, 1946, cote C-65, p. 2.

65. See Anthony Eden, *Memoirs*, vol. 2, *The Reckoning* (Boston, 1965), p. 432; inquiries regarding this question and a dossier

on Rossé addressed to the Historical Branch of the U.S. State Department, the Diplomatic Branch of the National Archives, the Military Branch of the National Archives, and the Franklin D. Roosevelt Memorial Library at Hyde Park, New York, produced no results. For Rossé's attempt to contact the Americans in 1940, see Justice, M-et-M., Dossier Rossé, liasse no. VII, audition de M. Postal, Raymond, le 17 décembre, 1945, cote C-32, p. 3.

66. Justice, M-et-M., Dossier Rossé, liasse no. IV, unnumbered and unaddressed letter dated June 12, 1941, cote 45, pièce 2; liasse no. IV, La brigade des affaires d'Alsace-Lorraine, no. 765, le 18 novembre, 1941, cote 45, pp. 1–5.

67. Ibid., liasse no. II, Le Général d'armée Huntziger . . . à M. le Maréchal de France . . . le 6 août, 1941, cote C-1.

68. Lettre du royaliste Jean Eschbach au maurrasien Calzant, Poligny, le 10 novembre, 1942, Arch. H-R, Coll. Heitz, cote 2J 213.62, pp. 8–9; Professor X., "Journal," January 3, 1941, p. 3; July 31, 1940, p. 31.

69. Justice, M-et-M., Dossier Rossé, liasse no. VII, procès-verbal de l'audition de M. Nominé, Henri, le 22 novembre, 1945, cote C-7, p. 2.

70. Ibid., liasse no. VII, procès-verbal de l'audition de M. Keppi, Jean, le 1 décembre, 1945, cote C-16, pp. 1–4; procès-verbal de l'audition de M. Brogly, Médard, le 11 janvier, 1946, cote C-55, annexe 3, pp. 1–4; procès-verbal de l'audition de M. l'abbé Gromer, Georges, le 1 février, 1946, cote C-79, pp. 1–2; déposition du témoin Zemb, Joseph, le 11 février, 1946, cote C-91, pp. 5–6.

71. Ibid., procès-verbal de l'audition de M. Brogly, Médard, le 11 janvier, 1946, cote C-55, p. 3.

72. Justice, Procès Stürmel, dossier no. 1, III, chemise no. 2, cote 405.

73. "Deutschstämmiger Elsässer," ibid., dossier no. 1, III, chemise no. 2, An den Herrn SS/Gruppenführer Kaul, den 1 Oktober, 1940, cote 409.

74. "Mein Lebenslauf," ibid., cotes 403–8.

75. Ibid., dossier no. 2, III (Scellés), scellé no. 2, pièce 11, Abschrift von Unterschäden, die nach dem 1.1.1926 entstanden sind; Professor X., "Journal," March 6, 1943, p. 461.

76. Justice, Procès Stürmel, dossier no. 1, III, chemise no. 2, procès-verbal de déposition de M. Joog, Louis, le 16 mai, 1946, cote 232.

77. Ibid., déposition du témoin Mourer, J-P., le 28 août, 1946, cotes 354–55.

78. Ibid., procès-verbal d'interrogatoire du nommé Stürmel, Marcel, 13 février, 1946, cotes 387–88; procès-verbal de l'audition du nommé Wagner, Robert, le 27 février, 1946, cote 8.

79. Ibid., Marzell Stürmel an den Gauleiter Robert Wagner, Reichsstatthalter und Chef der Zivilverwaltung im Elsass, den 3 März, 1943, cote 391; ibid., dossier no. IV (pièces parvenues à la Cour après la clôture de l'instruction), Der Chef der Zivilverwaltung im Elsass, Nr. Gö/St. 35 an Marzell Stürmel, den 13 April, 1943, pièce 1.

80. Ibid., dossier no. 1, VI (annexes de Me. Obringer en la cause contre Marcel Stürmel . . .), chemise no. 2, attestation de Julien Kraehling, avocat, le 6 septembre, 1946, pièce 14.

81. Ibid., IV, Assemblée nationale, le Secrétaire général de la questure, note sur la situation de M. Stürmel, ancien député de la 16e. législature, undated, pièce 12; see also, ibid., III, chemise no. 2, 16e. interrogatoire du nommé, Stürmel, Marcel, le 8 novembre, 1946, cotes 490–91.

82. Ibid., dossier no. 1, IV, paiements à M. Stürmel, Marcel, député, du 1er septembre, 1939, au 30 septembre, 1941, pièce 11.

83. Justice, Procès Bickler, III, chemise no. 2 (Réquisitoire), Information du nommé Wagner, le 11 mai, 1946, cote 15, pp. 1–2; Bundesarchiv, R. 57, DAI 817, box no. 17 (Elsass, 5–9), cote 40/3621.

84. Justice, Procès Bickler, liasse no. 3, chemise no. 3, scellé no. 1, pièces 1, 7, 11, 35, 58. Bickler's application for party membership (7.848.355) included a proof of German descent (Ahnentafel).

85. Ibid., pièce 54; Bickler's SS number was 367.776.

86. Ibid., liasse no. 3, chemise no. 3, scellé no. 2, An der Befehlshaber der Sicherheitspolizei des S. D., SS-Oberführer Dr. Scheel, den 11 November, 1940, pièces 1, 2.

87. Ibid., Der Komm. Kreisleiter an den Befehlshaber der

Staatspolizei, SS-Standartenführer Dr. Fischer, den 30 Mai, 1941, pièce 8, p. 2; the S. D.'s thanks for Bickler's services are in ibid., Der Sicherheitspolizei, Einsatzkommando III/1, An den Kr. Bickler, den 1 November, 1941, pièces 32, 34.

88. Ibid., liasse no. 3, chemise no. 3, II (unnumbered folder), procès-verbal no. 112 du 31 janvier, 1946, cote 5.

89. Bickler's letter of amnesty is in Bundesarchiv, R. 83, Nr. 33 (Meldungen der Staatspolizei Strassburg über staatsfeindliche Vorkomnisse und Aktionen sowie Abwehr derselben, 1941–1944), Der Kreisleiter an der Chef der Zivilverwaltung im Elsass . . . Robert Wagner, den 12 Januar, 1941, no. 327885.6, pp. 1–2.

90. Justice, Procès Bickler, liasse no. 3, chemise no. 3, I, scellé no. 2, Kreisleitung der NSDAP, Rundschreiben, den 6 März, 1941, pièces 42, 43; An. der Komm. Ortsgruppenleiter der NSDAP Herrn Renatus Kleinhans, Mommenheim, den 13 März, 1941, pièce 38. See also, An den Komm. Ortsgruppenleiter der NSDAP Fritz Zimmermann, Hochfelden, den 13 März, 1941, pièce 39.

91. Ibid., III, scellé no. 3, Der Kreisleiter, An den stellv. Gauleiter Pg. Röhn, den 14 März, 1942, Vertraulich; pièces 4–5, p. 3.

92. Ibid., liasse no. 3, chemise no. 2, undated (probably autumn 1942), unnumbered cote (printed propaganda sheet).

93. The Strasbourg party's displeasure is recorded in ibid., liasse no. 3, chemise no. 2, Information du nommé Röhn, Hermann, le 9 février, 1946, cote 8, p. 2; see also the account by Dr. Erich Isselhorst, commander of the Sicherheitspolizei and S. D. in Alsace from 1940 to 1944, "Das Elsass im dritten Reich: Betrachtungen aus der politisch-polizeilichen Perspektive," typescript, La Citadelle prison, Strasbourg, June 1947 (confidential source), pp. 1–93.

94. Justice, Procès Bickler, liasse no. 3, chemise no. 2, Direction générale des études et recherches, le 16 janvier, 1946, cote 6, pp. 1–5; procès-verbal de la déposition du témoin Dupin, Rolf, ex-chef de l'Abteilung IIIb du S. D. de Metz, le 12 février, 1946, cote 10, pp. 1–2.

95. Ibid., procès-verbal de la déposition du témoin Dupin, Rolf . . . le 12 février, 1946, cote 10, pp. 1–2.

96. Ibid., Direction générale des études et recherches, le 16 janvier, 1946, cote 6, p. 5.
97. Justice, Procès Spieser, III, chemise no. 3 (Service régional des renseignements généraux, Affaire c/ Spieser, Frédéric . . .), II, scellé no. 1, pièce 25.
98. *Strassburger Monatshefte* 4, no. 1 (October 1940): 174; Justice, Procès Spieser, III, chemise no. 3, I, unnumbered folder, pièce 2.
99. Justice, Procès Spieser, III, chemise no. 3, II, scellé no. 1, pièce 11; chemise no. 3, I, unnumbered folder, pièce 27, dated November 1, 1941.
100. Ibid., III, chemise no. 1, Fragebogen der Kreisleitung Zabern. Anlage zum Antrag auf Aufnahme in die NSDAP, cote 7; Fragebogen zur politischen Beurteilung, Streng vertraulich, den 9 April, 1942, signed by Kreisleiter Rudi Lang, cote 5, pp. 1–2; ibid., chemise no. 4 (Indemnité pour les dommages subis lors de la lutte pour le germanisme en Alsace par Spieser, Frédéric [Entschädigung für Volkstumschäden]), Schaden durch die Franzosen bis Mitte 1939, den 13 Mai, 1941, pièces 5–10.
101. Ibid., chemise no. 4, Der Zivilverwaltung im Elsass, Wiedergutmachung, An den Chef der Zivilverwaltung im Elsass, den 17 April, 1943, pièces 18–19; for the Hünenburg-Alsatia affair, see note 54, this chapter.
102. Ibid., chemise no. 1, Information du 11 mai, 1946, du nommé Wagner, Robert, cote 24, p. 1; the appeals for official intervention are in ibid., chemise no. 4, An den Herrn Staatsminister Pflaumer, den 20 Juli, 1943, pièces 23–24.
103. Ibid., chemise no. 1, Spieser an den SS-Oberstürmführer Dr. Schmitt, Buchsweiler [Bouxwiller], den 20 November, 1943, cote 14.
104. Ibid., chemise no. 3, II, scellé no. 1, pièces 15–24.
105. Spieser's expostulations are found in ibid., chemise no. 4, An den Herrn Staatsminister Pflaumer, den 20 Juli, 1943, pièces 23–24; the quote from Rossé's board is in ibid., chemise no. 4, Vermögenschäden aus dem Volkstumkampf im Westen an den Herrn Dr. F. Spieser, den 4 Januar, 1944, pièce 28. To the very end of the war, payments were made by the Germans to those Alsatians in Germany damaged by

the *Commissions de triage* from 1919 through 1925: these settlements totaled 250,000RM for the fiscal year 1944–45. See Bundesarchiv, R. 83, Nr. 72, Ermittlung der elsässischen Volkstumkämpfer, unnumbered cote.

106. Spieser, "Die Ehre des Elsasses," *Strassburger Monatshefte* 5, no. 7 (April 1942): 37–54; see also, Professor X., "Journal," April 11, 1942, p. 323.

107. Justice, Procès Spieser, III, chemise no. 3, II, scellé no. 1, pièces 15–24; chemise no. 1, Information contre Spieser, Frédéric, du nommé Wagner, Robert, le 27 avril, 1946, cote 24, pp. 1–2.

108. See Professor X., "Journal," August 13, 1941, p. 230.

109. Justice, Procès Mourer, III, chemise no. 1, Interrogatoire sur charges du nommé Mourer, J-P., le 7 janvier, 1947, cote C-18, pp. 31–39; chemise no. 4 (Activité de Mourer comme Kreisleiter), Tätigkeitbericht des Komm. Kreisleiters Pg. Hans Peter Murer, den 25 Februar, 1941, cote C-4, pp. 33–34.

110. Ibid., chemise no. 7 (articles de journaux concernant Mourer), cote vii, C-8; chemise no. 6 (attitude de Mourer à l'occasion des déportations et de l'incorporation des jeunes Alsaciens dans l'armée allemande), cote vi, C-25, p. 2; chemise no. 4, dépositions des témoins Delabre, Louis, et During, Pierre (confrontation avec Mourer, J-P.), le 16 décembre, 1946, cote iv, C-64, pp. 1–4; chemise no. 6, déposition du témoin Oser, Eugène (confrontation avec Mourer, J-P.), le 28 octobre, 1946, cote iv, C-20, pp. 1–5.

111. Ibid., chemise no. 1, Interrogatoire sur charges, p. 49; chemise no. 9 (témoins à décharge), procès-verbal de l'audition de Hennera, Joseph, le 20 novembre, 1946, cote ix, C-6; déposition du témoin Brogly, Médard, le 20 novembre, 1946, cote ix, C-11, pp. 1–4; déposition de Stürmel, Marcel, le 20 novembre, 1946, cote ix, C-12, p. 2.

112. Professor X., "Journal," January 23, 1942, p. 437; for anecdotes on Mourer's personal life, see July 25, 1942, p. 353; for his marital entanglements, see Justice, Procès Mourer, II (Bulletin no. 2 et renseignements), bulletin de renseignements, le 12 novembre, 1946, cote 2.

113. Justice, Procès Mourer, II, chemise no. 8 (activité de Mourer

après la libération de Mulhouse), procès-verbal de l'audition de Jordan, Jean, le 15 mai, 1946, cote viii, C-8, p. 3.

114. Ibid., chemise no. 4, procès-verbal de l'audition de Wagner, Robert, le 12 avril, 1946, cote iv, C-9, p. 2; chemise no. 8, procès-verbal de la déposition du témoin Wust, Charles, le 5 novembre, 1946, cote viii, C-4.

115. Déf. nat., Procès Ernst, liasse no. 2, procès-verbal d'interrogatoire ou de confrontation du nommé Ernst, Robert, le 2 juillet, 1947, cote 461, pp. 1–3.

116. Ibid., Direction départementale des services de police du Bas-Rhin, no. LD 3823, le 22 avril, 1947, cote 479, pp. 1–3; procès-verbal d'interrogatoire ou de confrontation du nommé Ernst, Robert, le 18 juillet, 1947, cote 493, pp. 3–4; procès-verbal de la déposition de Muller, Georges, le 2 septembre, 1947, cote 506, pp. 1–2. The young conscript later lost the use of one eye and received a war disability pension of 80 percent.

117. Ibid., liasse no. 3, Notes d'audience, Affaire Ernst, audience du 12 janvier, 1955, cote 738, p. 16; liasse no. 2, procès-verbal d'information du nommé Bilger, Joseph, le 11 juillet, 1947, cote 465, p. 4; liasse no. 1, procès-verbal de la déposition du témoin Stürmel, Marcel, le 8 avril, 1947, cote 234, p. 5.

118. Bundesarchiv R. 83, Nr. 41 (Berichte des S. D.-Führers Strassburg vom 17 Mai, 1944, bis 9 November, 1944), (Stimmungs-und Meinungsbildung im Elsass), Bericht vom 14.6. 1944, pp. 3–4; Bericht vom 21.8.1944, p. 2; Bericht vom 30.8.1944, pp. 1–2; Bericht vom 30.10.1944, p. 1; Bericht vom 4.11.1944, pp. 2–4.

119. Germany, Bundesarchiv (Coblenz), R. 70, Deutsche Polizeidienststellen im Elsass-Lothringen, Nr. 123, Abgesandte Fernschreiben des Gestapos Strassburg . . . November 1944, pp. 6–16.

120. Déf. nat., Procès Ernst, liasse no. 2, procès-verbal d'interrogatoire ou de confrontation du nommé Ernst, Robert, le 17 juillet, 1947, cote 471, pp. 1–3; procès-verbal de la déposition de M. Woerth, Christian, le 27 janvier, 1947, unnumbered cote, pp. 3–6.

CHAPTER 5

1. Justice, Procès Bickler, liasse no. 3, chemise no. 3, I, scellé no. 2, pièces 12, 15.

2. Justice, M-et-M., Dossier de Nancy, liasse no. I (Information devant le Tribunal militaire jusqu'en juin, 1940), A-forme, cote la.

3. *Le Républicain du Haut-Rhin*, April 25, 1946, p. 1.

4. Déf. nat., Procès Wagner, liasse no. 2 (Duplicata, Affaire Wagner et consorts), scellé no. 4, pièce 4, p. 4.

5. Déf. nat., Procès Ernst, liasse no. 2, procès-verbal d'interrogatoire ou de confrontation du nommé Ernst, Robert, le 18 juillet, 1947, cote 493, pp. 8-9.

6. Justice, Procès Mourer, liasse no. III, chemise no. 4, Interrogatoire du nommé Mourer, cote 1, C-8, p. 2.

7. Ibid.; chemise no. 1 (Information, procès-verbal de première comparution . . .), Le Directeur départemental des services de police du Bas-Rhin à M. Blaser, Juge d'instruction près la Cour de justice du Bas-Rhin [sic], section de Mulhouse, le 28 novembre, 1946, cote 1, C-9.

8. Ibid., chemise no. 4, déposition du témoin Ernst, Robert (confrontation avec Mourer, J-P.), le 11 décembre, 1946, cote iv, C-66, p. 9.

9. Ibid., chemise no. 1, procès-verbal de l'exécution d'un mandat d'arrêt concernant le nommé Mourer, J-P., le 24 juillet, 1946, cote 91, pp. 1-2.

10. Justice, Procès Bickler, liasse no. 1 (pièces de forme), Cour de justice du Bas-Rhin, section de Strasbourg, Cabinet d'instruction no. 10, Mandat d'arrêt, le 8 décembre, 1945, un-numbered cote; Spieser, *Tausend Brücken*, pp. 922-67.

11. Déf. nat., Procès Wagner, liasse no. 1, Colonel C. B. Mickelwait, JAGD, to Judge Charles Furby, Directeur général de la Justice . . . à Baden-Baden, le 13 novembre, 1945, cote 44; ibid., procès-verbal d'interrogatoire ou de confrontation du nommé Wagner, R., le 7 février, 1946, cote 132, p. 8; le 5 février, 1946, cote 128, p. 8.

12. Déf. nat., Procès Ernst, liasse no. 1, procès-verbal d'information, le 8 août, 1946, cote 28, pp. 1-2.

13. Justice, Procès Mourer, chemise no. 12, procès-verbal d'audi-

ence (publique) de la Cour de justice du Haut-Rhin, sous-section de Mulhouse, Affaire Mourer, J-P., le 26 février, 1947, cote 53g, 52g.

14. Ibid., questions posées à la Cour de Justice, Affaire contre le nommé Mourer, J-P., le 28 février, 1947, cote 65g.

15. Ibid., Cour d'appel de Colmar, Parquet général, no. 46/47, le 22 mars, 1947, unnumbered cote, pp. 1–6; Direction générale de la Sûreté nationale, no. 1014/47, Ste. 2891/47, procès-verbal d'inhumation concernant les nommés Ball, Ulrich, et Mourer, J-P., le 10 juin, 1947, pp. 1–2; the information regarding "national indignity" is taken from Peter Novick, *The Resistance versus Vichy: The Purge of Collaborators in Liberated France* (New York, 1969), pp. 146–49.

16. Justice, M-et-M., Dossier Rossé, liasse no. IX (Interrogatoire récapitulatif), unnumbered cote, p. 6.

17. *Le Républicain du Haut-Rhin,* June 10, 1947, p. 2 (testimony given the previous day).

18. Ibid., June 10, 1947, p. 2; June 11, 1947, p. 2.

19. *Dernières Nouvelles de Strasbourg,* June 13, 1947, pp. 1–2; the special characteristics of court judgments in Alsace as compared to the rest of France are discussed in Novick, *Resistance versus Vichy,* p. 164 n. 13.

20. *Le Républicain du Haut-Rhin,* October 27, 1951, p. 1.

21. Justice, Procès Stürmel, dossier no. 1, I (Pièces de forme), le Directeur de prisons [*sic*] de Fresnes à M. le Procureur de la République, 2e. section, le 19 décembre, 1945, cote 13.

22. Ibid., dossier no. 1, II (Bulletin no. 2 et renseignements), Cour de Justice du Haut-Rhin, sous-section de Mulhouse, no. 172/65, le 12 novembre, 1945, cote 1.

23. Ibid., dossier no. 1, III, no. 2, procès-verbal du 2e. interrogatoire de Stürmel, Marcel, le 30 avril, 1946, cote 473, p. 2; dossier no. 1, V (Règlement et pièces de procédure), Questions à la Cour de justice de Mulhouse, affaire: Stürmel, Marcel, le 18 juillet, 1947, pièce 31.

24. *Le nouveau Rhin français* (Mulhouse), August 22, 1947, p. 7.

25. Justice, Procès Stürmel, dossier no. 1, VII (Requête de Stürmel, Marcel, concernant imputation d'internement administratif), le Commissaire du Gouvernement près la Cour de justice du Haut-Rhin, sous-section de Mulhouse, à M.

le Procureur Général près la Cour d'appel à Colmar, le 13 février, 1950, unnumbered pièce.

26. Ibid., VIII (Affaire Stürmel, Marcel: Dossier d'amnistie), Cour d'appel séant à Colmar, La Chambre des mises en accusation no. 16/54 du 16 mars, 1954, unnumbered pièce.

27. Déf. nat., Procès Ernst, liasse no. 1, Tribunal militaire de Metz, Réquisitoire introductif, parquet 6130/304, le 7 mars, 1947, cote 40; liasse no. 3, Extrait des minutes du Greffe de la Cour d'Appel de Nancy, le 13 janvier, 1954, Affaire Ernst c/ Ministère Public, cote 673/D, pp. 1–3.

28. Ibid., liasse no. 3, piecès de forme, lettre de l'Amicale des anciens déportés politiques des camps de Schirmeck et du Struthof-Natzwiller (Bas-Rhin), le 31 janvier, 1954, cote 133.

29. Ibid., Cour d'appel de Colmar, Chambre détachée à Metz, Parquet général J. 92/54, Réquisitoire, le 9 mars, 1954, cote 691, pp. 1–8; République française, Cour de cassation, Chambre criminelle, le 30 juin, 1954, cote 675, pp. 1–2.

30. Ibid., Extrait des minutes de la Cour de cassation, no. 3190, le 16 novembre, 1954, cote 696, pp. 1–4; Tribunal militaire permanent des forces armées de Metz, Notes d'audience, Affaire Ernst, audience du 13 janvier, 1954, cote 738, p. 17.

31. Justice, Procès Bickler, liasse no. 3, chemise no. 4, I (Arrêt, demandes d'extradition, poursuites de l'affaire Bickler, 1947 à 1951), Extrait des minutes du Greffe de la Cour de justice du Bas-Rhin, Strasbourg, no. C.J. 5073/45, le 4 septembre, 1947, unnumbered cote; M. le Procureur Général près la Cour d'appel à Colmar, à M. le Directeur des services de police judiciaire, Paris, le 11 décembre, 1951, unnumbered cote.

32. Ibid., chemise no. 4, I, Le Commissaire de la République française en Allemagne à M. R. Schumann, Ministre des Affaires Etrangères, Cab. no. 6153 HC/CAB, le 8 septembre, 1950, unnumbered cote; M. J. Tarbe de Saint-Hardouin à M. R. Schumann, Ministre des Affaires Etrangères, no. 58/CH, le 11 mai, 1949, unnumbered cote; Cour d'appel de Colmar, Parquet du Procureur général à M. le Commissaire du Gouvernement près la Cour de justice à Strasbourg, no. 6841/48, très urgent, le 10 septembre, 1951, unnumbered cote.

33. Ibid., chemise no. 4, III (Commandement régional de la 6e. région militaire . . . Brigade des recherches de Sarreguemines, correspondance et procès-verbaux, 1961–63), procès-verbal d'enquête préliminaire, le 12 juin, 1961, unnumbered cote, pp. 1–5.

34. Ibid., Le Commandant de la Compagnie de gendarmerie de Sarreguemines au Commandant de la Compagnie de gendarmerie à Strasbourg, Bulletin de correspondance B 9-284/63, le 8 février, 1963, unnumbered cote.

35. Interview, M. le Bâtonnier S., Strasbourg, July 12, 1972.

36. Justice, Procès Spieser, III, chemise no. 2 (Ordonnances, citations à l'accusé), Extraits de minutes du Greffe de la Cour de justice de Strasbourg, no. C.J. 6038/45, le 3 septembre, 1947, unnumbered cote; Le maire de Strasbourg à M. le Commissaire du Gouvernement auprès de la Cour de justice, section du Bas-Rhin, le 7 août, 1947, unnumbered cote; République française, Mairie de Dossenheim-zur-Zinsel, le 6 octobre, 1947, unnumbered cote; Tribunal de première instance, Strasbourg, no. C.J. 5038/45, le 4 octobre, 1947, unnumbered cote (confiscation of property).

37. Ibid., chemise no. 1, Le Directeur général de la Sûreté nationale . . . à M. l'Administrateur général adjoint pour le Gouvernement militaire de la zone française d'occupation en Allemagne, le 5 juillet, 1946, cote 29; see also, Spieser, *Tausend Brücken*, pp. 922–67.

38. Justice, Procès Spieser, III, chemise no. 5 (Au sujet de Flick, Jeanne, actuellement internée au Camp de Struthof), Préfecture du Bas-Rhin, Arrêt, le 12 janvier, 1946, unnumbered cote.

CHAPTER 6

1. Justice, M-et-M., Dossier Rossé, liasse no. IX (Interrogatoire récapitulatif), unnumbered cote, pp. 60–62.

2. See Kettenacker, *Nationalsozialistische Volkstumspolitik*, p. 104.

3. "Communiqué," Mouvement régionaliste d'Alsace-Lorraine (Strasbourg), November 15, 1970, p. 1.

4. *L'Alsace* (Colmar), January 8, 1971; cf. the Alsace-Lorraine

Regionalist Movement's reply to these protests of André Bord, Pierre Messmer, and Emile Bourgeois in *Dernières Nouvelles de Strasbourg*, January 10, 1971, p. 5.

5. "Appel aux citoyens et aux autorités en Alsace et en Lorraine. Nous voulons garder notre langue," tract, Cercle René Schickelé (Strasbourg), 1972.

6. Jean-Jacques Mourreau, "Les problèmes de l'Alsace d'aujourd'hui." *Dossiers de l'histoire* 4 (July-September 1976): 76–77; this account estimates that the present "electoral base" of the autonomists is between 10 and 30 percent of the total voting population in Alsace.

7. *Elsa* [Journal bilingue d'action alsacienne-lorraine et européenne fédéraliste; Kampfblatt für Muttersprache, Heimatrecht und Europäischen Föderalismus] 15 (October 1972): 1.

8. "Movement régionaliste d'Alsace-Lorraine, E-L. [Elsass-Lothringen]," tract, May 13, 1972, signed Mlle. Bleyer.

9. Mourreau, "Les problèmes," p. 77.

10. Paul Schall, *Elsass, gestern, heute und morgen?* (Filderstadt-Bernhausen, 1976), pp. 55, 58, 65, 109, 116, 130, 159–62. Schall's preference goes to a doctoral thesis by Karl-Heinz Rothenberger, *Die elsass-lothringische Heimat- und Autonomie bewegung zwischen den beiden Weltkriegen* (Frankfurt-am-Main: Verlag Herbert Lang, 1975). I did not use this book in my study.

11. See Yves Mény, *Centralisation et décentralisation dans le débat politique française, 1945-1969* (Paris, 1974), pp. 121–22, 127; see also, Pierre Branche, "L'économie: un début d'émancipation," and Jacques Fleury, "Maintenir le cohésion nationale," *Le Figaro*, December 4, 1975, p. 2.

12. See Max Clos and Yves Clau, "Les Français entre la rogne et l'espoir, enquête: de la querelle franco-allemande au contentieux Alsace-Paris," *Le Figaro*, June 8, 1972, p. 5; June 9, 1972, p. 27.

13. Zvi Gitelman, *Jewish Nationality and Soviet Politics: The Jewish Section of the CPSU, 1917–1930* (Princeton, N.J., 1972), pp. 502 n. 22, 508 n. 27.

14. See Pierre Maugué, *Le particularisme alsacien, 1918–1967* (Paris, 1970), p. 260.

Bibliography

My list of source materials is divided in the following way:

1. Private Papers
2. Official Documents
   Unpublished
   Published
3. Books and Articles

1. Private Papers

Haenggi, Charles. "Mémoires. Drittes Buch: Kampfjahre im Elsass, 1926–1939." Dairies, Colmar, n.d. [1950].

Isselhorst, Dr. Erich. "Das Elsass im dritten Reich: Betrachtungen aus der politisch-polizeilichen Perspektive." Manuscript, confidential source, written in La Citadelle prison, Strasbourg, June 1947.

Wilsdorf, Christian. "Les incidents provoquées à Kaysersberg et à Orbey par les conseils de révision, les 14 et 15 février, 1943." Typescript, Archives du Haut-Rhin, Colmar, 1960.

X., Professor. "Journal de guerre, 1940–1945." Manuscript, confidential source, Colmar, 1940–1945.

2. Official Documents: Unpublished

France
Ministère d'Etat chargé des Affaires culturelles. Archives Nationales, Paris.

173

Section moderne. F⁷. Police générale. III. Alsace-Lorraine.
Cote F⁷ 13400. Liasse no. 2. Pièces 415 à 1047. Presse
d'Alsace-Lorraine (1926–1930). Journal autonomiste *Die
Zukunft* (1927–1929).
Cote F⁷ 13401. Pièces 1 à 616. Mouvement autonomiste:
rapports généraux, 1929–1930.
Cote F⁷ 13997. Mouvement autonomiste: rapports généraux
(procès de Colmar). 1928, avril-novembre.

The following series from the Section moderne, F⁷, Police
générale, of the Archives Nationales were not available at the
time research for this book was being conducted, but much
of the information contained in these files is duplicated in
the dossiers of the various trials (listed below) and in the
series below headed, Archives du Bas-Rhin, Strasbourg, No.
AL 98. Verzeichnis der "Valot-Akten" (Direction générale des
services d'Alsace-Lorraine à Paris).

Cote F⁷ 13390. Rapport sur la propagande séparatiste et
la question des minorités nationales (rapport du commissaire spécial de Strasbourg en date du 15 novembre,
1928).
Cote F⁷ 13395. Mouvement autonomiste (1925–1927).
Cote F⁷ 13396. Mouvement autonomiste. Janvier-décembre,
1928. Attentat contre le procureur général Pachot, 1928.
Heimatbund, manifeste, 1926.
Cote F⁷ 13398. Autonomisme. Rapports sur Rossé, 1929–
1931.
Cote F⁷ 13399. Autonomisme. Notes générales, 1932–1933.
Cote F⁷ 13403. Autonomisme. Rapports généraux, juin-
décembre, 1931.

Ministère d'Etat chargé de la Défense nationale. Direction de
la Gendarmerie et de la Justice militaire. Justice militaire. Dépôt
central des archives. Caserne Noëfort, Meaux, Seine-et-Marne.
Tribunal permanent des Forces Armées de Metz. Inventaire
des pièces de la procédure contre le nommé, Ernst, Robert
Frédéric, né le 4.2.1897 à Hurtigheim (Bas-Rhin), ex-
maire de la ville de Strasbourg et Generalreferent du
Gauleiter d'Alsace.

Liasse no. 1: Enquête préliminaire, cotes 1 à 3. Instruction, première partie, cotes 1 à 274.

Liasse no. 2: Instruction, deuxième partie, cotes 275 à 625.

Liasse no. 3: Instruction, troisième partie et notes d'audience, cotes 626 à 738.

Pièces de forme, nos. 1–133.

Pièces annexes dans la procédure suivie contre le Docteur Robert Ernst, dossiers 1–13. Liasse no. 1: Inventaire. C/1–C/13.

Tribunal militaire permanent de la 10e. région militaire séant à Strasbourg. Inventaire des pièces de la procédure suivie contre le nommé Wagner, Robert, sujet allemand, ex-Gauleiter d'Alsace, inculpé de recrutement illégal de la force armée au profit d'une puissance étrangère.

Liasse no. 1: pièces 1 à 145.

Liasse no. 2: duplicata Affaire Wagner et consorts. Scellés ouverts, nos. 1–13.

Liasse no. 3: Notes d'audience, le 23 avril, 1946–3 mai, 1946.

Ministère de la Justice. Cour de justice, section du Bas-Rhin. Chambre d'instruction no. 10. (Archives du Haut-Rhin, Colmar, cote des archives 32267.) Procès de Bickler, Armand Christian, 41 ans, avocat, inculpé du chef d'intelligence avec l'ennemi.

Liasse no. 1: Pièces de forme, unnumbered cotes, 32 total.

Liasse no. 2: Renseignements, unnumbered cotes, 3 total.

Liasse no. 3: Pièces d'information:

Chemise no. 1: L'activité de Bickler avant septembre, 1939. Cotes 1 à 87.

Chemise no. 2: Réquisitoire, mandat d'arrêt, procès-verbaux, interrogatoires de l'Affaire Bickler, cotes 1 à 35.

Chemise no. 3: Service régional des renseignements généraux, Strasbourg. Affaire c/ Bickler, Hermann, ex-Kreisleiter de Strasbourg, SS-Standartenführer inculpé d'intelligence avec l'ennemi.

Scellé no. 1: contenant des pièces numerotés de 1 à 69. Procès-verbal no. 112, du 31 janvier, 1946.

Scellé no. 2: contenant des pièces numérotés de 1 à 45. Procès-verbal no. 112, du 31 janvier, 1946.

Unnumbered folder, contenant des pièces numérotés de 1 à 36. Procès-verbal no. 112, du 31 janvier, 1946.

Unnumbered folder. Procès-verbal de recherches, de saisie, et de transmission des documents no. 112, du 31 janvier, 1946. Unnumbered cotes.

Chemise no. 4:

I. Arrêt, demandes d'extradition, poursuites de l'Affaire Bickler, 1947 à 1951. Unnumbered cotes.

II. Publications et notifications de l'Affaire Bickler, 1947 à 1960. Unnumbered cotes.

III. Commandement régional de la Gendarmerie de la VIIe. région militaire. VIe. Légion. Groupement de la Moselle . . . Brigade des recherches de Saareguemines. Correspondance et procès-verbaux, 1961–63. Unnumbered cotes.

Ministère de la Justice. Cour de justice du Haut-Rhin. Sous-section de Mulhouse. Chambre d'instruction no. 4. (Archives du Haut-Rhin, Colmar, cote des archives 34127.) Procès de Mourer, Jean-Pierre, 49 ans, ex-Kreisleiter de Mulhouse.

Liasse no. I: Pièces de forme, cotes 1 à 93.

Liasse no. II: Bulletin de renseignements, cotes 1 à 5.

Liasse no. III: Pièces d'information.

Chemise no. 1: Information, procès-verbal de première comparution, premier interrogatoire de curriculum vitae. Interrogatoire sur charges. Cotes 1 à 19.

Chemise no. 2: Rapports et pièces concernant le mouvement autonomiste. Cotes 1 à 8.

Chemise no. 3: Activité de Mourer avant 1940. Cotes 1 à 75.

Chemise no. 4: Activité de Mourer comme Kreisleiter. Cotes 1 à 81.

Chemise no. 5: Activité de Mourer comme remplacant du Kreisleiter de Ribeauvillé.

Chemise no. 6: Attitude de Mourer à l'occasion des déportations et de l'incorporation des jeunes Alsaciens dans l'armée allemande. Cotes 1 à 37.

Chemise no. 7: Articles de journaux, concernant Mourer. Cotes 1 à 11.

Chemise no. 8: Activité de Mourer après la libération de Mulhouse. Cotes 1 à 12.

Chemise no. 9: Témoins à decharge. Cotes 1 à 15.

Chemise no. 10: Copies de pièces. Unnumbered cotes.

Chemise no. 11: Pièces arrivées après la clôture de l'information. Cotes 1 à 62.

Chemise no. 12: Procédure devant la Cour de justice. Règlement. Cotes 1 à 84.

Ministère de la Justice. Archives départementales de Meurthe-et-Moselle, Nancy. Dossier contre Rossé, Joseph Victor.

Dossier de Nancy:

Liasse no. I. Information devant le Tribunal militaire jusqu'en juin, 1940.

Liasse no. II. Information reprise en juin 1945 devant le Tribunal militaire de Nancy, puis devant la Cour de Justice de Meurthe-et-Moselle.

Dossier Rossé:

Liasse sans numéro: pièces de forme.

Liasse no. I: Renseignements.

Liasse no. II: Pièces d'information.

Liasse no. III: Pièces concernant la détention.

Liasse no. IV: Pièces à conviction.

Liasse no. V: Mémoires produites par Rossé pour sa défense.

Liasse no. VI: Interrogatoires.

Liasse no. VII: Témoins.

Liasse no. VIIa: Témoins à décharge concernant les démarches de Rossé.

Liasse no. VIII: Conférences.

Liasse no. IX: Interrogatoire récapitulatif.

Dossier Alsatia:

Liasse no. I: Pièces de forme.

Liasse no. II: Pièces à conviction.

Liasse no. III: Témoins.

Liasse no. IV: Interrogatoires.

Ministère de la Justice. Cour de justice, section du Bas-Rhin. Chambre d'instruction no. 10. (Archives du Haut-Rhin, Colmar, cote des archives 32298.) Procès de Spieser, Frédéric, 43 ans, château de la Hunabourg, inculpé d'intelligence avec l'ennemi.

Pièces de forme, unnumbered cotes, 25 total.
Renseignements, unnumbered cotes, 5 total.
Pièces d'information:
>   Chemise no. 1: L'activité de Spieser avant et pendant la
>   guerre. Cotes 1 à 38.
>   Chemise no. 2: Ordonnances, citation à l'accusé, unnum-
>   bered cotes, 10 total.
>   Chemise no. 3:
>> Unnumbered folder. Service régional des renseignements
>> généraux, Strasbourg. Affaire c/ Spieser, Frédéric . . .
>> Pièces jointes, numérotées de 1 à 33 (procès verbal no.
>> 123 en date du 12 avril, 1946).
>> Scellé no. 1, contenant des pièces numérotées de 1 à 31
>> (procès-verbal en date du 12 avril, 1946).
>> Unnumbered folder. Au sujet de Ernst, Robert . . . Pièces-
>> jointes numérotées de 1 à 28 (procès-verbal no. 120/4
>> en date du 12 juin, 1946 [sic]).
>   Chemise no. 4: Indemnité pour les dommages subis lors
>   de la lutte pour le germanisme en Alsace par Spieser
>   [Entschädigung für Volkstumsschäden].
>   Chemise no. 5: Au sujet de Flick, Jeanne, actuellement in-
>   ternée au Camp de Struthof.

Ministère de la Justice. Cour de justice du Haut-Rhin. Sous-
section de Mulhouse. Tribunal de première instance de Mulhouse. Chambre d'instruction no. 1. (Archives du Haut-Rhin,
Colmar, cote des archives 34131.) Procès de Stürmel, Marcel
René, 46 ans, ancien député d'Altkirch, inculpé du chef d'intelligence avec l'ennemi et atteinte à la sûreté extérieure de l'Etat.
Dossier no. 1 (741 de classement de Mulhouse).
>   Pièces de forme, cotes 1 à 17.
>   Bulletin no. 2 et renseignements.
>   Pièces d'information:
>> Chemise no. 1: Dossier du tribunal militaire de Nancy,
>> cotes 1 à 37.
>> Chemise no. 2: Pièces d'information, cotes 2 à 504. Inter-
>> rogatoires. Mémoires de l'inculpé . . . [1939–1947].
>   Pièces parvenues à la Cour après la clôture de l'instruction,
>   cotes 1 à 72.

Règlement et pièces de procédure, cotes 1 à 42.
Annexes:
  Annexes de Me. Obringer en la cause contre Stürmel, Mar-
    cel, ancien député d'Altkirch. Unnumbered pièces, 30
    total [1943–1954].
  Annexes de Me. Obringer en la cause contre Stürmel, Mar-
    cel, ancien député d'Altkirch. Pièces 1 à 50 [1940–
    1947].
Cour de justice du Haut-Rhin. Sous-section de Colmar.
  Requête de Stürmel, Marcel, concernant imputation
  [sic] d'internement administratif. Audience du 23
  mars, 1950. Rejet.
Affaire Stürmel, Marcel, René. Dossier d'amnistie [1953–
  1954].
Dossier no. 2 (742 de classement de Mulhouse).
Chemises:
  Chemise no. 1: Journaux d'avant 1940 et de 1945.
  Chemise no. 2: Extraits de journaux, 1940–1941, cotes
    1 à 18.
Dossiers 1 et 2 de contributions directes de Stürmel, Marcel.
Scellés:
  Service régional des renseignements généraux à Strasbourg.
    Scellé no. 1, contenant des pièces numérotées de 1 à
    41. (Procès-verbal no. 121 du 4 avril, 1946.)
    Scellé no. 2, contenant des pièces numérotées de 1 à 17.
    (Procès-verbal du 4 avril, 1946.)
    2e. Scellé no. 1, contenant des pièces numérotées de 1 à
    24. (Procès-verbal en date du 24 juin, 1946.)
    Unnumbered scellé. Dossier pièces jointes numérotées
    de 1 à 4. (Procès-verbal en date du 24 juin, 1946.)
  Direction général de la Sûreté nationale. Affaire contre
    Stürmel, Marcel. . . .
    Scellé no. 1, contenant 34 pièces cotées de 1 à 34.
    Mulhouse, le 14 janvier, 1946.
    Scellé no. 3 [sic], contenant 13 pièces cotées de 1 à 13.
    Mulhouse, le 15 janvier, 1946.
    Scellé no. 4, contenant 14 pièces cotées de 1 à 14. Mul-
    house, le 15 janvier, 1946.

Archives du Bas-Rhin, Strasbourg.
No. AL 98. Verzeichnis der "Valot-Akten" (Direction générale
   des services d'Alsace-Lorraine à Paris). Paquets 634–95 and
   1278–95.
No. AL 140. Bordereau des dossiers provenant du Commissariat Général de la République à Strasbourg et de la
   Haute-Commission interalliée des territoires rhénans, 1919–
   1939. 8 paquets, 57 dossiers.

Archives du Haut-Rhin, Colmar.
Cour d'appel de Colmar. Le procès des autonomistes. Date
   de versement: 6 mars, 1970. Cotes des archives 35791–804.
Inventaire de la sous-série 2 J. Collection Fernand-Joseph
   Heitz. Date de versement: 1968.

Germany
Auswärtiges Amt, Bonn. Politisches Archiv. Büro des Staats-
sekretärs.
No Aktenzeichen. Autonomiebewegung in Elsass-Lothringen.
   No Band number. Datum 3.27–4.30. (U.S. National Archives,
   Series T-120/serial 2277–78.)
Politische Abteilung II. Elsass-Lothringen. Politik 5A. Die
   Stellung Elsass-Lothringens im französischen Staate, hierin
   auch die Elsass-Lothringische Autonomiefrage. Band 1–18.
   Datum 3.20–1.36. (U.S. National Archives, Series T-120,
   serials 5361–62.)
Politische Abteilung II. Elsass-Lothringen. Autonomisten.
   Autonomisten-Bewegung in Elsass-Lothringen. Band 1. Da-
   tum 5.22–12.23. (U.S. National Archives, Series T-120, serial
   5363.)
Politische Abteilung II. Elsass-Lothringen. Politik 26. Po-
   litische und Kulturelle Propaganda. Band 1. Datum 3.20–
   7.32. (Not microfilmed.)
Politische Abteilung II. Elsass-Lothringen. Politik 29. Faschis-
   mus. Band 1. Datum 12.33–3.34. (Not microfilmed.)
Politische Abteilung II. Elsass-Lothringen. Politik 5. Innere
   Politik, Parlaments- und Parteiwesen. Band 1. Datum 3.20–
   10.36. (U.S. National Archives, Series T-120, serial 5360.)
Politische Abteilung II. Elsass-Lothringen. Politik 2. Pol-

itische Beziehungen zu Deutschland. Band 1. Datum 3.20–
6.36. (U.S. National Archives, Series T-120, serial 5360.)

Auswärtiges Amt, Bonn. Politisches Archiv. Geheimakten 1920–
1936. Länder II.

Frankreich. Politik 5. Elsass-Lothringen: Die Stellung Elsass-
Lothringen in französischen Staat, sowie die Elsass-Lothrin-
gische Autonomiefrage. Band 1–3. Datum 5.20–9.35. (U.S.
National Archives, Series T-120, serial 2804.)

Frankreich. Politik 15. Elsass-Lothringen: Agenten und
Spionagewesen. No Band numbers. Datum 8.27–5.36. (Not
microfilmed.)

Inland II. Geheim. No Aktenzeichen. Inhalt: Politisches
Berichte Rumänien, Serbien . . . Elsass-Lothringische Frage.
Datum 1943. (U.S. National Archives, Series T-120, serial
4204.)

Neue Reichskanzlei. No Aktenzeichen. Elsass-Lothringen. No
Band numbers. Datum 1940–1943. (U.S. National Archives,
Series T-120, serial 735.)

Neue Reichskanzlei. Auswärtiges Amt. Elsass-Lothringen. No
Band numbers. Datum 1933–1936. (U.S. National Archives,
Series T-120, serial 3141.)

Politische Abteilung II. Po 36. Elsass-Lothringen. Inhalt:
Judenfrage. No Band numbers. Datum 5.38–7.38. (U.S.
National Archives, Series T-120, serial 4356.)

Politische Abteilung II. Politisches Verschluss (Geheim). Po
g Frankreich. Deutsch-französische Abkommen vom 6.12.38.
No Band numbers. Datum 2.38–2.39. (U.S. National Archives, Series T-120, serials 912, 1854.)

Bundesarchiv, Coblenz.

Series T-253. serials 36–39, 42, 49. Der Nachlass Karl Haus-
hofer.

Der Nachlass Rudolf Pechel. Teil I. Nr. 124–26 (1921–1932).

Der Nachlass Hans Steinacher.

R. 57. Deutsches Ausland-Institut, Stuttgart, DAI 165, 816–18,
888. (Dr. R. Czaki, Elsass-Lothringen.)

R. 58. Reichssicherheitshauptamt. Der Reichsführer-SS und
Chef der deutschen Polizei. Der Chef der Sicherheits-

polizei und des S. D. Amt III. Meldungen aus dem Reich. Geheim!

R. 70. Deutsche Polizeidienststellen in Elsass-Lothringen.

Nr. 29. Verbeugende Verbrechensbekämpfung, allgemeines, insbesondere Massnahmen im Elsass, 1940–1942.

Nr. 30, Band 5. April-Juni 1942.

Nr. 41. Finanzielle Bedienung und Versorgung von V-Personen . . . S. D. Angehörigen und Vollzugsbeamten des SIPO, 1942–1944.

Nr. 47. Berichte an des BdS Baden/Elsass, insbesondere über Frontverlauf, Sicherheitspolizeiliche Lage, Evakuierungen, Schanzarbeiten. Dezember 1944–Januar 1945 (Kolmar).

Nr. 49, Band 7. Februar 1943–Februar 1944.

Nr. 51, Band 6. August-Dezember 1942.

Nr. 76. Absiedlung von elsässischen Familien . . . 20.11.1944.

Nr. 80, Band 1. Dienststellengebäude des S. D.-Strassburg und seine Aussenstellen . . . volks- und reichsfeindlichen Vermögen . . . 1941–1944.

Nr. 100. Beschäftigung von V-männern bei den Gendarmerie, allgemeines. Oktober 1943.

Nr. 123. Abgesandte Fernschreiben des Gestapos Strassburg . . . November 1944.

Nr. 132. Uberführung männliches und weibliches Häftlinge im Sicherungslager Vorbruck bei Schirmeck und die Konzentrationslager Natzweiler und Ravensbrück . . . April-Juni 1943.

Nr. 133. Sicherung des Betriebe gegen feindliche Spionage . . . 16.9.1944. Festnahmen wegen illegale Grenzübertritte . . . Einzelfälle.

R. 83. Elsass: Zentrale Stellen der allgemeine Zivilverwaltung im 2. Weltkrieg im Elsass. (Der Reichsstatthalter in Baden und Chef der Zivilverwaltung im Elsass.)

Nr. 8. Meldungen von Sabotagefällen, 1942–1944.

Nr. 27. Reden des Gauleiters und Reichsstatthalters Robert Wagner, 1940–1944.

Nr. 29. Elsässer in der französischen Armee—Ubersichten der französischen Offiziere in Heer und Luftwaffe mit deutsch klingende Familiennamen. 1942.

Nr. 33. Meldungen des Sicherheitspolizei Strassburg über staatsfeindliche Vorkommnisse und Aktionen sowie Abwehr derselben. 1941–1944.

Nr. 34. Einsetzung der Kreisleiter der NSDAP im Elsass und Aufstellung der Schaltsfestsetzung. 1940–1942.

Nr. 37. Behandlung elsässischer Frage durch französische Behörden bezw. Presse. 1941–1943. (Erklärung des Marschalls Pétain. . . .)

Nr. 41. Berichte des SD-Führers Strassburg über die Stimmungs- und Meinungsbildung im Elsass für die Zeit vom 17 Mai, 1944, bis 9 November, 1944.

Nr. 72. Ermittlung der elsässischen Volkstumkämpfer und deren Unterstützung nach ihrer Befreiung aus französischen Haft. 1940–1944.

Nr. 81. Verbot des Tragens, Herstellens und Verkauf von französischen Uniformstücken sowie von Baskenmützen und dergleichen. 1940–1944.

Official Documents: Published

France

Journal officiel de la république française, 1870–1940, Chambre des députés 1876–1940: Débats parlementaires, compte rendu in extenso, 11 janvier 1881–4 juin 1940. Paris: Imprimerie des journaux officiels, 1881–1940.

Journal officiel de la république française, 1870–1940, Sénat 1876–1940: Débats parlementaires, Compte rendu in extenso, 11 janvier 1881–21 mai 1940. Paris: Imprimerie des journaux officiels, 1881–1940.

Germany

Verordnungsblatt des Chefs der Zivilverwaltung im Elsass. 4 vols. Strasbourg: Strassburger Neueste Nachrichten, 1940–44.

3. Books and Articles

"Alsace et Lorraine. Terres françaises." *Cahiers du témoignage chrétien,* October-December 1943, pp. 1–96.

Baas, Geneviève. *Le malaise alsacien, 1919–1924.* Strasbourg: Journal developpement et communauté, 1972.

Baechler, Christian. *Les Alsaciens et le grand tournant de 1918.*
Strasbourg: Journal developpement et communauté, 1972.

Bailliard, Robert. "Historique du repatriement des Alsaciens incorporés de force." *Saisons d'Alsace* 39–40 (summer-autumn
1971): 473-83.

Bené, Charles. *L'Alsace dans les griffes nazies.* Vol. 1, *Honneur
et Patrie.* Vol. 2, *L'Alsace dans la Résistance française.* Vol.
3, *L'Alsace dans la Résistance française, II.* Raon l'Etape:
Fetzer, 1971, 1973, 1975.

Berstein, Serge. "Une greffe politique manquée: le radicalisme
alsacien de 1919 à 1939." *Revue d'histoire moderne et contemporaine* 17 (January-March 1970): 78–103.

Bickler, Hermann. *Widerstand: Zehn Jahre Volkstumkampf der
Elsass-Lothringische Jungmannschaft.* Strasbourg: Hünen-
burg-Verlag, 1943.

Binoux, Paul. *Les pionniers de l'Europe, L'Europe et le rapprochement franco-allemand: J. Caillaux, A. Briand, R.
Schumann, K. Adenauer, J. Monnet.* Paris: C. Klincksieck,
1972.

Boberach, Heinz. *Meldungen aus dem Reich: Auswahl aus den
geheimen Lageberichten des Sicherheitsdienstes der SS,
1939-1944.* Neuwied and Berlin: Hermann Luchterhand,
1965.

Bonnet, Serge. *Sociologie politique et religieuse de la Lorraine.*
Paris: A. Colin, 1972.

Boosz, Alphonse; Cogniot, Georges; et al. *Analyse de l'Alsace.*
Paris: Editions de la nouvelle critique, 1955.

Bopp, Marie-Joseph. *L'Alsace sous l'occupation allemande, 1940–
1945.* Le Puy: Xavier Mappus, 1945.

Brongniart, Philippe. *La région en France.* Paris: A. Colin,
1971.

Cairns, John C. "International Politics and the Military Mind:
The Case of the French Republic, 1911-1914." *Journal of
Modern History* 25 (September 1953): 272–85.

Cernay, Louis. *Le maréchal Pétain, l'Alsace et la Lorraine: Faits
et documents (1940-1941).* Paris: Les îles d'or, 1955.

Cézard, Pierre. "L'annexion de fait de l'Alsace et de la Lorraine,
juin, 1940-septembre, 1942." *Revue d'histoire de la 2e. guerre
mondiale* 2, no. 4 (January 1952): 37–52.

Charbonneau, Henry. *Les mémoires de Porthos.* Paris: P. Desroches, 1969.

Clauser, Marthe. *Statistique de la déportation dans le Haut-Rhin, 1940-1945.* Colmar: Préfecture du Haut-Rhin, 1964 (ronéotypé).

Clement, G-R. *Avec l'Alsace en guerre (1940-1944).* Paris: Librairie Istra, 1945.

Conquet, Général Alfred. *Auprès du maréchal Pétain.* Paris: Editions France-Empire, 1970.

Dansette, Adrien. *Religious History of Modern France.* Vol. 2, *Under the Third Republic.* Translated by John Dingle. New York: Herder and Herder, 1961.

Das Elsass von 1870 bis 1932: Herausgegeben im Auftrag der Freunde des Abbé Dr. Haegy von J. Rossé, M. Stürmel, A. Bleicher, F. Dieber, J. Keppi. 4 vols. Colmar: Verlag Alsatia, 1932.

Delperrie de Bajac, Jacques. *Histoire de la milice, 1918-1945.* Paris: Fayard, 1969.

De l'Université aux camps de concentration: Témoignages strasbourgeois. Paris: Les belles lettres, 1947.

Déniel, Alain. *Le mouvement breton, 1919-1945.* Paris: Maspero, 1976.

Deutsch, Karl W. *Nationalism and Social Communication: An Inquiry into the Foundations of Nationality.* 2nd ed. Cambridge, Mass.: M.I.T. Press, 1969.

Dollinger, Philippe. "Du royaume franc au Saint-Empire." In *Histoire de l'Alsace,* edited by Philippe Dollinger, pp. 57–84. Toulouse: Privat, 1970.

―――. "Le déclin du moyen âge." In *Histoire de l'Alsace,* edited by Philippe Dollinger, pp. 133–70. Toulouse: Privat, 1970.

Dreyfus, François G. *La vie politique en Alsace, 1919-1936.* Paris: A. Colin, 1969.

Eccard, Frédéric. *Mes carnets, 1939-1940: Avec les Alsaciens évacués en Périgord.* Strasbourg: Editions des Dernières Nouvelles, 1952.

Eden, Anthony. *Memoirs.* Vol. 2, *The Reckoning.* Boston: Houghton Mifflin, 1965.

Ernst, Robert. *Rechenschaftsbericht eines Elsässers*. Berlin: Bernard und Graefe, 1954.

Ford, Franklin. *Strasbourg in Transition, 1648–1789*. Cambridge, Mass.: Harvard University Press, 1958.

Foville, Jean-Marc de. *La collaboration*. Paris: Culture, art, loisirs, 1969.

Freymond, Jean. "Les industriels allemands de l'acier et le bassin minier lorrain (1940–1942)." *Revue d'histoire moderne et contemporaine* 19 (1972): 27–44.

Gatzke, Hans W. *Germany's Drive to the West (Drang nach Westen)*. Baltimore: Johns Hopkins Press, 1950.

Gitelman, Zvi. *Jewish Nationality and Soviet Politics: The Jewish Section of the CPSU, 1917–1930*. Princeton, N.J.: Princeton University Press, 1972.

Granier, Jacques. *Et Leclerc prit Strasbourg*. Strasbourg: Editions des Dernières Nouvelles, 1970.

Haelling, Gaston. *Une préfecture désannexée: Strasbourg, 23 novembre 1944–8 mai 1945*. Strasbourg: Editions Le Roux, 1954.

Hansi. *See* Waltz, Jean-Jacques.

Hatt, Jean-Jacques. "La préhistoire." In *Histoire de l'Alsace*, edited by Philippe Dollinger, pp. 11–26. Toulouse: Privat, 1970.

————. "L'Alsace romaine." In *Histoire de l'Alsace*, edited by Philippe Dollinger, pp. 27–56. Toulouse: Privat, 1970.

Heiber, Helmut, ed. *Reichsführer: . . . Briefe an und von Himmler*. Stuttgart: Deutsche Verlags-Anstalt, 1968.

Heitz, Robert. *A mort (souvenirs)*. Paris: Editions de Minuit, 1946.

————. *Souvenirs de jadis et de naguère*. Woerth: Imprimerie de Woerth, 1963.

Herrenschmidt, Suzanne. *Mémoires pour la petite histoire: Souvenirs d'une Strasbourgeoise*. Strasbourg: Istra, 1973.

Herriot, Edouard. *Jadis*. Vol. 2, *D'une guerre à l'autre, 1914–1936*. Paris: Flammarion, 1952.

Himly, François-Joseph. *Bibliographie alsacienne, 1937–1950*. Paris-Strasbourg: Editions le Roux, 1951.

————. *Bibliographie alsacienne, 1951–1960*. Dijon: Imprimerie Bernigaud et Privat, 1954–62.

———. "Bibliographie alsacienne." *Revue d'Alsace* 100 (1961): 151–94 [bibliography for 1960]; 101 (1962): 152–93 [bibliography for 1961]; 103 (1965): 109–93 [bibliography for 1962–64].

Hitler, Adolf. *Mein Kampf.* Vol. 1, *Eine Abrechnung.* Vol. 2, *Die nationalsozialistische Bewegung.* Munich: Zentralverlag der NSDAP, Franz Eher Nachf., 1938.

———. *Tischgespräche im Führerhauptquartier, 1941–1942.* Edited by Percy E. Schramm, with A. Hillgruber and A. Vogt. Stuttgart: Seewald Verlag, 1963.

Hoffet, F. *Psychanalyse de l'Alsace.* Paris: Flammarion, 1951.

Hüttenberger, Peter. *Die Gauleiter: Studie zum Wandel des Machtgefüges in der NSDAP.* Stuttgart: Deutsche Verlags-Anstalt, 1969.

Jacobsen, Hans-Adolf. *Nationalsozialistische Aussenpolitik, 1933–1938.* Frankfurt-am-Main: Metzner Verlag, 1968.

———, ed. *Hans Steinacher, Bundesleiter des V.D.A. 1933–1937: Errinerungen und Dokumente.* Boppard-am-Rhein: Harald Boldt Verlag, 1970.

Jaeckel, Eberhard, *Frankreich in Hitlers Europa: Die deutsche Frankreichpolitik im zweiten Weltkrieg.* Stuttgart: Deutsche Verlags-Anstalt, 1966.

Jeanneney, Jules. *Journal politique: septembre, 1939–juillet, 1942.* Edited by Jean-Noël Jeanneney. Paris: A. Colin, 1972.

Kaul, Friedrich Karl. "Das SS- 'Ahnenerbe' und die 'jüdische Schädelsammlung' an der ehemaligen 'Reichsuniversität Strassburg.'" *Zeitschrift für Geschichtswissenschaft* 11 (1968): 1460–75.

Keller, Général Pierre. *Au temps de Staline: A la recherche des prisonniers libérés en U.R.S.S.* Paris: Editions du Scorpion, 1960.

Kent, George O. *A Catalog of Files and Microfilms of the German Foreign Ministry Archives, 1920–1945.* 4 vols. Stanford, Calif.: The Hoover Institution, 1962–72.

Kettenacker, Lothar. *Nationalsozialistische Volkstumspolitik im Elsass.* Stuttgart: Deutsche Verlags-Anstalt, 1973.

Krausnick, Helmut; Buchheim, Hans; Broszat, Martin; and Jacobsen, Hans-Adolf. *Anatomy of the SS State.* Translated by

Richard Barry, Marian Jackson, and Dorothy Long. New York: Walker and Co., 1968.

Kruuse, Jens. *Madness at Oradour, 10 June 1944 and After.* Translated by Carl Malmberg. London: Secker and Warburg, 1969.

La Mazière, Christian de. *Le rêveur casqué.* Paris: Laffont, 1972.

Lang, Madeleine. *Bibliographie alsacienne 1965–1966.* Strasbourg: Bibliothèque nationale et universitaire de Strasbourg, 1970 (ronéotypé).

Lassus, Jean. *Souvenirs d'un cobaye.* Colmar: Alsatia, 1973.

L'Huillier, Fernand. "L'évolution dans la paix (1814–1870)." In *Histoire de l'Alsace,* edited by Philippe Dollinger, pp. 395–432. Toulouse: Privat, 1970.

———. "L'Alsace dans le Reichsland (1871–1918)." In *Histoire de l'Alsace,* edited by Philippe Dollinger, pp. 433–68. Toulouse: Privat, 1970.

———. "L'Alsace contemporaine: un destin exceptionnel." In *Histoire de l'Alsace,* edited by Philippe Dollinger, pp. 469–500. Toulouse: Privat, 1970.

———. *Dialogues franco-allemands, 1925–1933.* Paris: Diffusion Ophrys, 1971.

———. *Libération de l'Alsace.* Paris: Hachette, 1975.

Livet, G. "Le 18e. siècle et l'esprit des lumières." In *Histoire de l'Alsace,* edited by Philippe Dollinger, pp. 305–56. Toulouse: Privat, 1970.

Maugué, Pierre. *Le particularisme alsacien, 1918–1967.* Paris: Presses d'Europe, 1970.

Marchese, Stelio. *La Francia ed il problema dei rapporti con la Santa Sede, 1914–1924.* Naples: Edizioni Scientifiche Italiane, 1969.

Marx, R. "De la pré-révolution à la restauration." In *Histoire de l'Alsace,* edited by Philippe Dollinger, pp. 357–94. Toulouse: Privat, 1970.

Mayeur, Jean-Marie. "Une bataille scolaire: les catholiques alsaciens et la politique scolaire du gouvernement du Front Populaire." *Cahiers de l'Association Interuniversitaire de l'Est* (1962), pp. 85–101.

———. *Autonomie et politique en Alsace: La Constitution de 1911.* Paris: A. Colin, 1970.

Meinecke, Friedrich. *Strassburg, Freiburg, Berlin, Erinnerungen.* Stuttgart: K. F. Koehler, 1949.

Meissner, Otto. *Elsass und Lothringen, deutsches Land.* Berlin: O. Stollberg, n.d. [1941].

Mény, Yves. *Centralisation et décentralisation dans le débat politique français, 1945–1969.* Paris: Librairie générale de droit et de jurisprudence, 1974.

Mey, Eugène [Capitaine Firmin]. *Le drame de l'Alsace, 1939–1945.* Paris: Berger-Levrault, 1949.

Michel, Henri. *Les courants de pensée de la Résistance.* Paris: Presses Universitaires de France, 1962.

———. *Bibliographie critique de la Résistance.* Paris: Institut pédagogique national, 1964.

Mièvre, Jacques. "Les débuts de 'l'Ostland' en Meurthe-et-Moselle." *Revue d'histoire de la 2e. guerre mondiale* 20, no. 79 (July 1970): 61–82.

Milward, Alan. *The New Order and the French Economy.* New York: Oxford University Press, 1970.

Mordrel, Olier. *Breiz Atao, ou l'histoire et l'actualité du nationalisme breton.* Paris: Alain Moreau, 1973.

Mourreau, Jean-Jacques. "Les problèmes de l'Alsace d'aujourd'-hui." *Dossiers de l'histoire* 4 (July-September 1976): 65–81. The entire issue is entitled "Régionalisme et francophonie."

Noguères, Henri, and Degliame-Fouché, Marcel. *Histoire de la Résistance en France.* 3 vols. Paris: Laffont, 1970.

Novick, Peter. *The Resistance versus Vichy: The Purge of Collaborators in Liberated France.* New York: Columbia University Press, 1969.

Ochs, Eugène. *Pardon sans oubli.* Strasbourg: Editions des Dernières Nouvelles, 1969.

Pange, Comte Jean de. *Journal.* Vol. 1, *1927–1930.* Paris: Grasset, 1964.

Paul, Harry. *The Second Ralliement: The Rapprochement between Church and State in France in the Twentieth Century.* Washington: Catholic University of America Press, 1967.

Paxton, Robert O. *Vichy France. Old Guard and New Order, 1940–1944.* New York: Knopf, 1972.

Perreau, Robert. *Avec Hansi à travers l'Alsace: Le livre du Centenaire de Hansi, 1873–1973.* Colmar: Alsatia, 1973.

Pflimlin, Pierre, and Uhrich, René. *L'Alsace, destin et volonté.* Paris: Calmann-Levy, 1963.

Pinson, Koppel. *Modern Germany: Its History and Civilization.* New York: Macmillan, 1954.

Plum, Günter. *Bibliographie der Gauleiter der NSDAP.* Munich: Institut für Zeitgeschichte, 1970.

Le procès du complot autonomiste de Colmar, 1–24 mai, 1928: comptes-rendus des débats (Où est le complot?). Colmar: Alsatia, 1928.

Rapp, F. "Discipline et prospérité, 1539–1618." In *Histoire de l'Alsace,* edited by Philippe Dollinger, pp. 219–58. Toulouse: Privat, 1970.

Redslob, Robert. *Entre la France et l'Allemagne: Souvenirs d'un Alsacien.* Paris: Plon, 1933.

Rich, Norman. *Hitler's War Aims.* Vol. 1, *Ideology, the Nazi State, and the Course of Expansion.* Vol. 2, *The Establishment of the New Order.* New York: Norton, 1973–74.

Sajer, Guy. *Le soldat oublié: Récit.* Paris: Laffont, 1967.

Sartre, Jean-Paul. *Les mots.* Paris: Gallimard, 1964.

Schaeffer, Eugène. *L'Alsace et la Lorraine, 1940–1945: Leur occupation en droit et en fait.* Paris: Librairie générale de droit et de jurisprudence, 1953.

Schall, Paul. *Zwei Jahre Aufbau im Elsass.* Strasbourg: Oberrheinischer Gauverlag und Druckerei, 1942.

———. *Elsass, gestern, heute und morgen?* Filderstadt-Bernhausen: Erwin von Steinbach Stiftung, 1976.

Schickelé, René. *Die Grenze.* Berlin: Rowohlt, 1932.

Schneider, Johann. *Die Elsässische Autonomistenpartei, 1871–1881.* Frankfurt-am-Main: Selbstverlag des Elsass-Lothringen Instituts, 1933.

Seager, Frederic H. "The Alsace-Lorraine Question in France, 1871–1914." In *From the Ancien Régime to the Popular Front: Essays in the History of Modern France in Honor of Shepard B. Clough,* edited by Charles K. Warner, pp. 111–26. New York: Columbia University Press, 1969.

Shafer, Boyd C. *Faces of Nationalism: New Realities and Old Myths.* New York: Harcourt, Brace, 1972.

Silverman, Dan P. *Reluctant Union: Alsace-Lorraine and Imperial Germany, 1871–1918.* University Park, Pa.: Pennsylvania State University Press, 1972.

Siwek-Pouydesseau, Jeanne. *Le corps préfectoral sous la 3e. et la 4e. républiques.* Paris: A. Colin, 1969.

Smith, Anthony D. *Theories of Nationalism.* London: Duckworth, 1971.

Spieser, Friedrich. *Kampfbriefe aus dem Elsass.* Berlin: Volk und Reich Verlag, 1941.

————. *Tausend Brücken: Eine biographische Erzählung aus dem Schicksal eines Landes.* Stuttgart: Neuer Hünenburg Verlag, 1952.

Spindler, Charles. *L'Alsace pendant la guerre.* Strasbourg: Librairie Treuttel et Würtz, 1925.

Stehlin, Général Paul. *Témoignage pour l'histoire.* Paris: Laffont, 1964.

Storck, Joachim. "René Schickelé, eine europäische Existenz." *Frankfurter Heft* 25 (1970): 577–88.

Stresemann, Gustav. *Vermächtnis, der Nachlass . . .* 2 vols. Berlin: Ullstein, 1932–33.

Thorez, Maurice. *Oeuvres.* 23 vols. Paris: Editions Sociales, 1950–65.

Tournoux, Général Paul-Emile. *Défense des frontières: Hautcommandement et gouvernement, 1919–1939.* Paris: Nouvelles éditions latines, 1960.

Umbreit, Hans. *Der Militärsbefehlhaber in Frankreich, 1940–1944.* Boppard-am-Rhein: Harald Boldt, 1968.

Vallat, Xavier. *Le nez de Cléopâtre: Souvenirs d'un homme de droite, 1918–1945.* Paris: Les quatre fils Aymon, 1957.

Vergnaud, P. *L'idée de la nationalité et de la libre disposition des peuples dans ses rapports avec l'idée de l'Etat, 1870–1950.* Paris: Domat-Montchrestien, 1955.

Waltz, Jean-Jacques [Hansi]. *Souvenirs d'un annexé récalcitrant.* Vol. 1, *Madame Bissinger prend un bain: Scènes de la vie à Colmar vers 1880.* Vol. 2, *Le premier phonographe: Lycée impérial de Colmar.* Mulhouse: L'Alsace, 1950.

Winock, Michel. "Socialisme et patriotisme en France, 1891–1894." *Revue d'histoire moderne et contemporaine* 20 (July–September 1973): 376–423.

Zahner, Armand. *Survivre à Tambow.* Mulhouse: Editions Salvator, 1970.

——. *Le soldat honteux: J'étais un "malgré-nous."* Mulhouse: Editions Salvator, 1972.

Ziegler, Janet. "Répertoire international des bibliographies publiées de 1945 à 1965 sur la seconde guerre mondiale." *Revue d'histoire de la 2e. guerre mondiale* 16, no. 63 (July 1966): 69–80.

——. "Bibliographies sur la seconde guerre mondiale." *Revue d'histoire de la 2e. guerre mondiale* 21, no. 81 (January 1971): 95–104.

Index